2/05

Oyster

Animal
Series editor: Jonathan Burt

Already published

Crow
Boria Sax

Ant
Charlotte Sleigh

Tortoise
Peter Young

Dog
Susan McHugh

Cockroach
Marion Copeland

Some forthcoming titles

Wolf
Garry Martin

Bear
Robert E. Bieder

Tiger
Susie Green

Spider
Katja and Sergiusz Michalski

Snake
Drake Stutesman

Parrot
Paul Carter

Bear
Robert E. Bieder

Whale
Joseph Roman

Falcon
Helen Macdonald

Rat
Jonathan Burt

Moose
Kevin Jackson

Hare
Simon Carnell

Fox
Martin Wallen

Bee
Claire Preston

Oyster

Rebecca Stott

REAKTION BOOKS

For JB

Published by
REAKTION BOOKS LTD
79 Farringdon Road
London EC1M 3JU, UK
www.reaktionbooks.co.uk

First published 2004
Copyright © Rebecca Stott 2004

Printed and bound in China

British Library Cataloguing in Publication Data

Stott, Rebecca
    Oyster. – (Animal)
    1. Oysters 2. Animals and civilization
    I. Title
    594.4

    ISBN 1 86189 221 7

Contents

A five-year old shellfish-worker in Biloxi, Mississippi, in 1911.

Prologue: On Oysters and Memory

In 1929 journalist and food writer Hector Bolitho described his love affair with the oyster in a delightful book called *The Glorious Oyster*. In colonial New Zealand, where he grew up in the late nineteenth century, settlers imitating English ways of life ate roast beef and Yorkshire pudding, shortbread from Edinburgh, turkey and steamed pudding at Christmas. Food was heavy, overcooked and rarely discussed or contemplated, for, Bolitho explains, by the nineteenth century talking about food had become a taboo: 'So the gourmet of Queen Victoria's time became a sinner. He met his kind in secret . . . '.[1] All this was to change for Bolitho when, at the age of fifteen, he went to stay in a boarding house in a hotel on a 'romantic' island off the coast of New Zealand, a mile or so from a settlement where Maoris were reputed to have eaten oysters at their cannibal feasts. Here the boy met a mysterious English traveller at the dining table and the two discovered a mutual pleasure in talking about food – oysters in particular. Eager to please the young man, Bolitho promised to take him to a rocky shore where oysters grew in their thousands:

We came upon a place where the oysters grew, packed together, as closely as grapes. My English companion put the basket on the ground. He was a smiling, good-looking fellow, with a shirt and collar cut so well that they filled me with envy. He opened the basket and took out two bottles, two glasses, two plates and two forks. I produced nothing but a chisel. I broke the oysters off, one by one, choosing the big ones of tidy shape. The outsides of their shells were still wet from the sea. We prised them open and placed them, eighteen upon each plate. My friend produced lemon and red pepper and I began to eat.

'Wait,' he said. He brought the two bottles from a place behind the rock, where they had been cooling in a pool. One was champagne, and the other was stout. And thus was I introduced to the pleasure of eating oysters with black velvet. The drink was two thirds of stout and one of champagne.

When I rush back over the years of my life, that summer day stands out as vividly as any. The calm, warm sea, the log against which we leaned, the plate of succulent fat oysters on my knee, and the first glass of this magic drink, which made the oysters more wonderful than any I had eaten before. And then my friend talked about food, of avocado pears dressed with vinegar and oil he had eaten in Africa, of stuffed lobsters – I remember the pleasure with which he described the colour of the red shell against the blue plate, as he had eaten them in Paris. He talked, too, of Russian soups, and fish stuffed with mushrooms, and duck dressed with yellow tiger lilies, snails perfectly cooked, brought out of their houses with the aid of a slender two-pronged silver fork.

'But the oyster is the loveliest of all food' . . . he said . . . 'Someday you must write in praise of the oyster.'

Oyster desires.

Bolitho describes a midsummer encounter on a shoreline which ends with a promise and then a parting, after which nothing will be the same again. This is an awakening – not only to taste but also to beauty and to language. The boy's promise to turn oysters into words for the mysterious stranger will be an act of love and of dedication to beauty. Bolitho's description of his first taste of oysters as a moment of transformation is often repeated, particularly by writers. Because the oyster inspires both revulsion and fascination, the action of putting a live oyster in the mouth is an act of courage, curiosity and trust for each new oyster eater – trust that others have been here before and not only lived but have acquired a taste for more. Not surprisingly, then, these memories of eating the first oyster are often remembered and recounted as rites of passage in which there is an initiator and an initiated. In eating the oyster the novice passes from one stage into another. The oyster often thus marks a passing and a moment of transition.

Unlike the mammals in this series, the oyster does not map onto the human form: it has no recognizable head, legs, eyes, mouth, skin, hands or arms. As a sea creature, it is quintessentially alien to the human form and to human experience. Yet when humans have anthropomorphized the oyster, it has been to describe the imagined essential forlornness of the oyster's condition: most often a combination of loneliness, mournfulness, melancholy, nostalgia and unrequited love. The oyster is usually described as closed to the world, sealed off, and thus to have suffered: as silent, solitary and secret as an oyster. And fascinatingly, though oysters, in common with other similar sea creatures, change their sex frequently, the anthropomorphized oyster is almost always male.

The history of the oyster–human encounter is a history characterized by intimacy and distance. They have been beyond knowing, beyond language, but as food they are also naked, exposed, offered up to be consumed and swallowed in millions in Roman villas on ancient seashores, and, in more modern times, in restaurants and from oyster stalls. The oyster tastes of the exotic, the salty unknown darkness of the sea-bed, yet its flesh is also strangely familiar; its name used as the title of one of the most notorious Victorian pornographic magazines, *The Oyster*, paired with its sister journal, *The Pearl*. Oysters are both on the tongue and beyond the power of the tongue. They are not only slippery; they are evasive, almost beyond knowing.

Like the other animals in this series, the oyster, through its relationship with humankind, has accumulated layers of meanings through time, not limitless, but particular. Oysters have been eaten by prehistoric humans and cultivated since the Romans in many ways and within infinitely varied contexts. More surprisingly, perhaps, they have been used to explore aspects of the human condition: greed, lust, flesh and pleasure in particular, but also, as one of the earliest life forms on the planet, they have been used to explore natural philosophical questions about 'deep time' and about the nature of life itself.

This book explores the oyster as a material being, its life history, reproductive modes and evolutionary history, its long association with sex in the human mind, the set of relationships it has had with man as food source since prehistoric times and the development of oyster and pearl industries around the world, as well as the rich meanings the oyster has amassed through time and in different cultures. What is the oyster and what has it come to be and mean alongside and for man? These questions need to be answered within specific contexts and with a long historical view. To tell the story of man's relationship with the oyster is to tell of railways, Dutch seventeenth-century still-life painters, oyster dredgers, oyster police and oyster thieves, gourmets and epicures, beachcombers, oyster acts and oyster bills, and to tell too of the philosophies, meditations, moral homilies and poetry the oyster has inspired since the beginning of human culture.

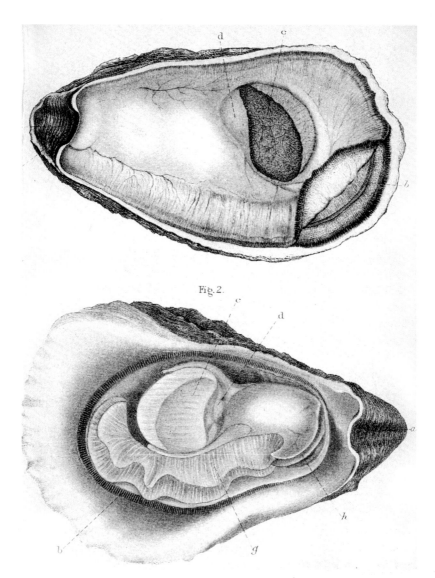

Fig. 2.

Anatomy of the oyster.

1 Oyster Biographies

Zoologically speaking, the oyster is a mollusc – an animal without a backbone but with an outer shell. It belongs to the same zoological phylum, Mollusca, as the mussel and snail and also the octopus and squid. It is also more precisely classified as a bivalve, which means that it has a shell in two parts or 'valves', held together by a hinge made of elastic ligament. But how has it come to be? How did the oyster 'become' an oyster? How *long* did it take for this curious anatomy – soft and complex, cupped in a hard shell lined with mother-of-pearl – to evolve?

OYSTER EVOLUTIONS

In *The Meaning of Evolution*, G. G. Simpson claims that 'an oyster of 200,000,000 or more years in the past would look perfectly familiar if served in a restaurant today'.[1] So we have to move even further back in time in order to trace its evolutionary beginnings. Zoologists speculating about the evolutionary origins of any creature begin by watching its embryological development, because the life cycle of an animal 'recapitulates' its evolutionary history like a kind of ancestral shadow. It is no coincidence that so many embryos of different creatures, including humans and oysters, look like sea creatures, for many of the first life forms on the planet were aquatic,

emerging out of a primal sea. Unlike other increasingly amphibious land species that crawled their way lumberingly or slitheringly on to dry land, the oyster found an ideal way of reproducing and feeding on the seabed. Then, over millions of years of natural selection, it perfected that *modus vivendi*.

Oysters and other bivalve molluscs descended from a common ancestor, a 'rather stocky' marine animal like the modern snail. This creature had most of its movement muscles concentrated in a kind of foot set at the back and would have moved over the sea-bed with its tentacled head extended, sieving seawater for food through a gill cavity near its 'foot'. Gradually – and we have to image time-lapse photography here stretching over thousands and millions of years of pre-history – it developed a sheet of tissue or a mantle, like the modern snail shell, to protect its soft flesh and – over more time – this developed into a dome-like shell. If alarmed it could retract both head and foot into this shell.

Then over yet more unimaginable stretches of time, the snail-shell-like mantle closed in, bending along the mid-line down the centre of the back to form two shells. At this point in its evolution the 'oyster' (if we can call it that) could protrude its 'foot' by pumping blood into it, and protract its head like the snail or tortoise, but, as its two shells thickened over time, strengthening its defence mechanisms, the oyster's head and foot became redundant and atrophied. The original gill cavity now came to extend all around the animal so that more and more water could be pulled through its body.[2] Now if it were to be served on a plate in a restaurant it would be recognized as an oyster.

Fossil remains confirm such speculations about the oyster's origins. The very first animals on earth were microscopic single-celled aquatic animals – like bacteria – which emerged around 3,200 million years ago (in the Precambrian era) and crowded the seas. By around 540 million years ago (the very beginning of the Cambrian period, called the Palaeozoic era), their successors, who all still lived in the sea, had evolved hard outer skeletons that shielded the vulnerable parts of their bodies. This armoury enabled the various groups to multiply and develop very quickly. The most successful of these 'armoured' animals were the arthropods (segmented animals with an outer skeleton) known as the trilobites, which were diversifying into many different forms allowing them to flourish in different conditions all around the world.

The illustration overleaf from *Life Before Man* (1972) shows some of the earliest forms of sea life: trilobites swim alongside echinoderms (spiny-skinned creatures – see the bulging bodies on a short stalk); the romantically named sea-lilies (far left) fan the water and brachiopods or 'arm-footed' creatures with two shells (bottom right) sift the water for plankton. Cephalopods (early relations of the cuttlefish) swim in tube-like shells, arms

An artist's impression of the 'armoured' life of the early seas. Oysters evolved from the brachiopods pictured on the sea-bed at bottom right.

appearing to sprout from their heads. The animals that had survived to this point in prehistory had evolved defence mechanisms, armour and shells, and vulnerable tentacled flesh was now retractable.

The fossil record shows that it was about 400 million years ago (the mid-Paleozoic era) that molluscs began to appear. Zoologists divide molluscs into three groups: gastropods (snails), bivalves (cockles, mussels and oysters – sea creatures with valves or shells, hinged together) and cephalopods (squid, octopus, cuttlefish and extinct groups such as ammonites and belemnites). Bivalves were particularly successful in ancient seas, gradually increasing in number

A book illustration of a placodont, an early predator of the oyster.

throughout the Mesozoic era and Tertiary period (between 225 and 65 million years ago) and diversifying in shape, size, colour, reproductive modes and means of protection. Some lived in mud, others cemented themselves to hard surfaces, a few could even swim.

Species of early oysters made their appearance amongst these diversifying bivalves around 200 million years ago (the upper Triassic period) and multiplied enormously for the next 70 million years (through the Jurassic and Cretaceous periods) so that by 135 million years ago they were one of the largest mollusc groups in the seas: an oyster empire.

In its earliest days, then, the oyster shared the seas with cephalopods (related to the modern octopus and cuttlefish), ammonites (creatures like cuttlefish which lived inside a spiralled many-chambered shell), belemnites (which had two gills and a spear-shaped inner shell), early corals, ray-finned fishes, sharks, sea urchins, jellyfish and starfish. But who were their predators? Who ate oysters before human time? Placodonts,

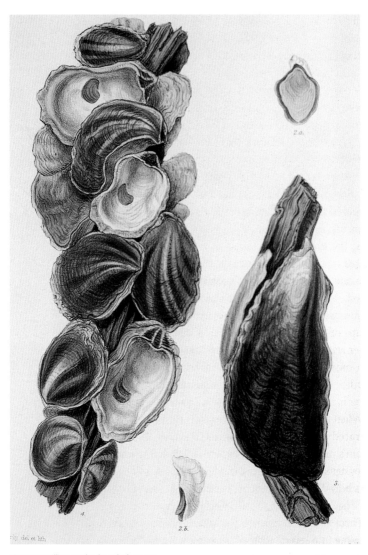

Ostrea cucillina or the hooded oyster.

marine reptiles that looked like walrus–turtle hybrids with three eyes, lived mainly on molluscs and oysters and had evolved teeth for tearing off the shells from the sea-bed rocks and grinding them, and a snout for searching out molluscs in the mud, like a pig seeking truffles. One of the first oyster eaters was, then, as close to the walrus as any other modern animal. Later, of course, Lewis Carroll would make much of his walrus oyster eater in 'The Walrus and the Carpenter', but we may never know if he knew of the walrus's placodont ancestor.

Oysters flourished in the age of the amphibious lizard and the dinosaur. On land, at the same time, other primitive armoured amphibians foraged, fought and reproduced: early forms of newts and salamanders, turtles and tortoises, crocodiles, the brontosaurus, diplodocus and brachiosaurus and winged reptiles. All of these reptiles would become extinct during a catastrophic change of climate at the end of the Cretaceous period, around 65 million years ago. Dinosaurs, ichthyosaurs, plesiosaurs, pterosaurs, belemnites, ammonites and many other groups of invertebrates and brachiopods died away. But the oyster was one of the survivors, outliving the catastrophe along with most other molluscs and crocodiles, tortoises, snakes, lizards, gastropods, octopi, cuttlefish and giant squid.[3] The oyster had out-survived the dinosaur.

When the Revd Williams mused in 1856 that the oyster 'is to be traced to a period so remote as to eclipse the ancestry of Britain's proudest peer',[4] his hyperbole fabulously understated the oyster's story, for these shellfish filtered the seas millions of years before *Homo sapiens* appeared some modest 130,000 years ago. The oyster is nearly 200 million years older than man.

Through that long history oysters continued to diversify, mutating into several different subgroups, adapting slowly and through natural selection to the conditions in which they lived.

Varieties of oyster. The names show attempts to make analogies with other natural objects: *Ostrea frons* or the leaflet oyster; *O. retusa* or the obsolete oyster; *O. quercinus* or the oak oyster.

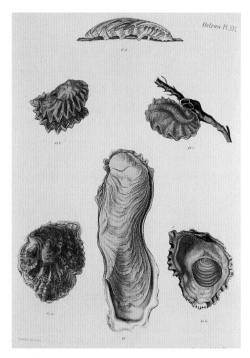

Those from colder regions evolved to fertilize within the oyster (these are called 'larviporous') and include the European oyster (*Ostrea edulis*), British Columbian (*Ostrea lurida*), Japanese (*Ostrea gigas*), South Australian and Tasmanian (*Ostrea angasi*), and New Zealand (*Ostrea chilensis*). Others adapting to warm and tropical seas evolved to spawn straight into the sea (they are called 'oviporous') and these include the US oyster (*Crassostrea virginica*), Japanese (*Crassostrea gigas*), Australian (*Crassostrea commercialis*), Portuguese (*Crassostrea angulata*) and Indian (*Ostrea cucullata*).

Eccentric oysters include rock oysters, giant coxcomb oysters, honeycomb oysters, thorny oysters and mangrove oysters.

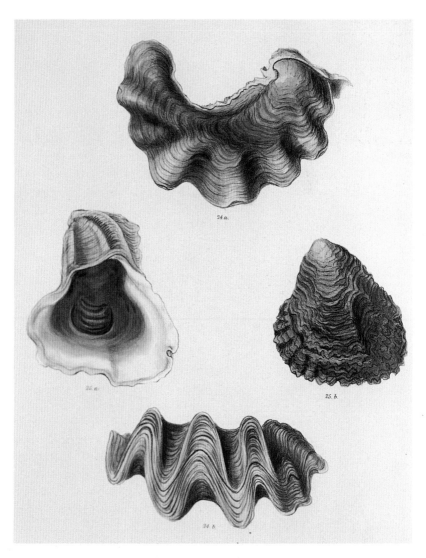

Ostrea megadon or large-toothed oyster, and *Ostrea rufa* or rufous oyster.

Ostrea crista or the gigantic oyster.

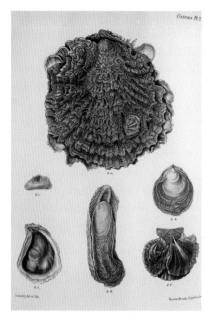

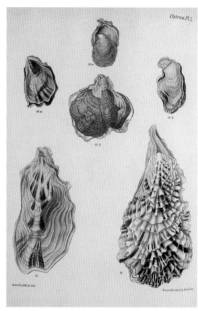

Pearl oysters come from a remote branch of the oyster family called *Pteriidae,* which are lined with the finest nacre or mother-of-pearl. The nacre is formed by the mantle of the oyster-shell, which extracts lime or calcium carbonate from the water; its function is simply to protect the soft flesh of the oyster from the rough shell. When a foreign object or parasite such as a bit of broken shell or grain of sand or a tiny worm, crab or fish gets inside the oyster-shell, the mantle secretes the nacre around it again to protect the soft flesh.

For most oyster eaters, however, the differences can be divided simply into two categories: the Pacific oyster (*Crassostrea* species, which is generally larger and has an oval shell) and the flat (native) oyster (*Ostrea* species, which is smaller and has a rounder shell). The tastes are different; prices differ. Flat

Ostrea edulis or the flat oyster.

A grouping of oysters:
Ostrea permollis,
O. ochracea,
O. rostralis and
O. talienwahnensis.

oysters are in great demand and more difficult to grow. Over the last century flat oysters have been struck by diseases and have been largely replaced on oyster-farms around the world by Pacific oysters or *Crassostrea gigas*. As the Pacific oyster spawns straight into the sea it can be controlled and cultivated more easily; in cooler climates the 'spat' or oyster larvae must be bred in artificial conditions and then transferred to the seabed.

OYSTER LIVES

The oyster is no butterfly or peacock. It has no bright colouring, plumage or charisma. Yet it is the most prolific and sexually fluid of all the sea creatures. Its fertility is a survival strategy, for whilst unimaginable numbers of oyster eggs and sperm are produced during the ejaculations of the oyster breeding season, each oyster that reaches an oyster stall or plate in a fine restaurant has done so against all odds, for only a few will survive the conditions of the seabed.

Oysters spawning, showing the smoky ejaculations of the breeding season.

24

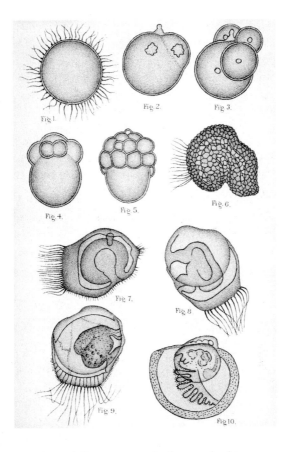

The oyster 'spat' or larva in its various stages of development.

Fig 1. Fig 2. Fig 3. Fig 4. Fig 5. Fig 6. Fig 7. Fig 8. Fig 9. Fig 10.

Ostrea species and *Crassostrea* species have evolved to reproduce in different ways. *Ostrea* species eggs are fertilized inside the parent oyster and *Crassostrea* species eggs are fertilized outside as sperm and egg clouds meet in sea water. Whichever way, the young larva or 'spat' swims about freely for about two weeks, 'his taste of vagabondage, of devil-may-care free roaming', writes food author, M.F.K. Fisher. She continues:

A bunch of oysters, showing growth of mussels and barnacles.

A set of oysters on a shell, showing crowding.

And even then they are not quite free, for during all his youth he is busy growing a strong foot and a large supply of sticky cementlike stuff. If he thought, he might wonder why . . . The two weeks up, he suddenly attaches himself to the first clean hard object he bumps into. His fifty million brothers who have not been eaten by fish may or may not bump into anything clean and hard, and those who do not, die. But our spat is lucky, and in great good spirits he clamps himself firmly to his home, probably forever.[5]

'Home' in the wild may be a rock, a mangrove tree, the post of a pier, even the shell of another oyster. In the nineteenth century a

26

Oysters growing on a stone.

Oysters growing on an old boot.

Mr Payne of Blackheath put together a collection of objects on which oysters had grown. These included a seventeenth-century champagne bottle thrown from the wreck of the *Royal George*, a Chinese teapot without a spout dredged up from the Falmouth River, inside which the oyster had grown to enormous size, and

several old sea-saturated boots.[6] If the oyster is a cultured oyster born into an oyster-farm, 'home' (the cultch laid down for the oysters to attach to) will depend upon where it is in the world: in France, for instance, it may be a lime-coated tile; in Japan, a submerged bamboo wigwam; or in a Norwegian sea fjord, it may be bundles of suspended birch twigs.

From this point, now firmly anchored, he devotes himself to feeding, pumping litres of seawater through his body and simultaneously straining it with his gills for plankton and other small organisms. For a human this would mean drinking the contents of 62 bathtubs every hour, or the contents of a large swimming pool between one dawn and the next. The water is pumped through the body by means of tiny hairs or cilia: 'a ciliated surface', writes C. M. Yonge, 'resembles a field of corn blown by the wind with waves of movement passing over it in the direction of the effective beat'.[7]

I use the masculine pronoun, as Fisher does, with some hesitation, for the oyster is never quite sexually fixed. It is generally

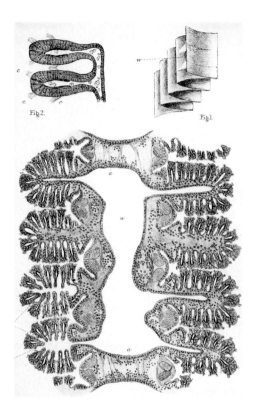

Oyster gills filtering seawater for plankton.

assumed that for the first year at least, the oyster is male, and fertilizes a few hundred thousand eggs in his first summer. But 'he' matures into femaleness: 'one day, maternal longings surge between his two valves in his cold guts and gills and all his crinkly fringes. Necessity, that well-known mother, makes him one. He is a she.'[8] But since around 50 per cent of the oyster population is female at any one point of the season, the female oyster must turn back to maleness from time to time.[9] It is now estimated that the oyster may change its sex up to four times a

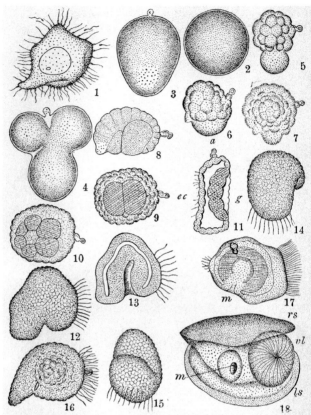

FIG. 1. Unfertilized egg shortly after mixture of spawn and milt; spermatozoa are adhering to the surface.

FIG. 2. Egg after fertilization.

FIG. 3. Same egg 2 minutes later. Polar body at broad end.

FIG. 4. Same egg 6 minutes later.

FIG. 5. About 6½ hours later.

FIG. 6. Another egg at about the same stage. Mass of small cells growing over large cell or macromere a.

FIG. 7. Egg 55 minutes later. Macromere almost covered by small cells of ectoderm.

FIG. 8. Optical section of egg 27 hours after impregnation, showing two large cells, derived from a in fig 5, covered by a layer of small ectodermal cells.

FIG. 9. Egg a few hours older, showing large cells viewed from below.

FIG. 10. An egg somewhat older viewed from above, showing further subdivision of large cells as seen through cells of upper layer.

FIG. 11. An older egg, now become flattened from above downward. Viewed in optical section.

FIG. 12. Surface view of an embryo just beginning to swim.

FIG. 13. Optical section of same.

FIG. 14. Surface view of same from another position.

FIG. 15. Surface view of same from another position.

FIG. 16. An older embryo in same position as in fig 12

FIG. 17. A still older embryo showing spherical ciliated digestive cavity opening by mouth, m.

FIG. 18. An embryo with well-developed larval shells, older than fig. 1, Plate VIII. rs, right shell; ls, left shell; vl, velum; m, mouth.

The development of the oyster.

year controlled by some mysterious synchronicity or the vagaries of water temperature or salinity. Perhaps, with all that seawater pumping through its body incessantly, it is at least poetically appropriate that it should be as sexually fluid as this. Ogden Nash wrote in 1931:

> The oyster's a confusing suitor
> It's masc., and fem., and even neuter.
> But whether husband, pal or wife
> It leads a painless sort of life.
> I'd like to be an oyster, say,
> In August, June, July or May.

The adult oyster has no head, limbs, eyes, nose, jaws or teeth, but it has a highly tuned sensory system that works like a radar and its anatomy, the nineteenth-century marine zoologist T. H. Huxley wrote, is 'greatly more complicated than a watch'.

Its body is shut between two concave limestone doors, which are hinged at one end, like a long cheque-book bound together at the back. An adductor muscle at the hinge opens and closes its shell and acts as a double locking device. Its radar system is sensitive to the slightest movement and dredgers report that even the shadow of their boats passing over oyster-beds will make them close up their shells. The shell increases in size and thickness season by season as the oyster secretes successive layers of pearlized lime over its inner surface, each layer no thicker than tissue paper. At three years old it is large enough to be eaten.

The oyster's radar and defensive mechanisms are critical for its survival, for mouths other than human mouths hunger for oyster flesh. Oysters have several principal predators: the starfish wraps its arms around the oyster, forces its shell apart and ingests it; the boring sponge bores tiny holes in its shell,

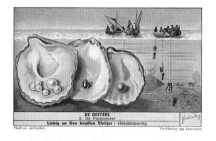

DE OESTERS
2. De Pareloester
Liebig en Oxo bouillon Blokjes : vleesbesparing
Nadruk verboden   Verklaring op keerzijde

DE OESTERS
1. Hoe een oester er zoal uitziet
Volledige toebereide Gerechten Liebig : juist gaar
Nadruk verboden   Verklaring op keerzijde

DE OESTERS
6. Oesterputten
Liebig Chicken Soup : de kippensoep met «Belgische» smaak
Nadruk verboden   Verklaring op keerzijde

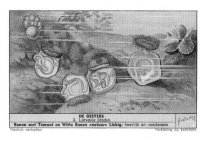

DE OESTERS
3. Larvaire Stadia
Bonen met Tomaat en Witte Bonen «natuur» Liebig : heerlijk en voedzaam
Nadruk verboden   Verklaring op keerzijde

DE OESTERS
4. Vijanden van de oesters : krab, zeester, boorslak
Lemco : klare en natuurlijke kippensoep
Nadruk verboden   Verklaring op keerzijde

DE OESTERS
5. Uitzetten van collecteurs
Liebig Groentenconserven : «natuurlijk» bereid
Nadruk verboden   Verklaring op keerzijde

This set of six German cards was given away by the Liebig Extract of Meat Company (LEMCO) in the 1950s.

honeycombing it with tunnels; the slipper-limpet and the mussel smother the oysters or starve them by attaching themselves to an oyster's shell and eating all their food; the dog-whelk and the whelk-tingle also bore into the shell and suck out the flesh. The oyster, beset by such enemies, writes M.F.K. Fisher, 'lives motionless, soundless, her own cold ugly shape her only dissipation, and if she escapes the menace of duck-slipper-mussel-

Black-Drum-leech-sponge-borer-starfish, it is for man to eat because of man's own hunger'.[10]

Starfish attacking oysters.

And if oysters have slowly evolved successful defence strategies to keep hungry predators out of their shells, their most ingenious predators continue to find new ways of getting in. Astonishingly, the French aquaculturist Yves LeBorgnes invented a mechanism for breeding oysters with pull-tabs in 1996. The pull-tab, called a 'Fizz', consists of a plastic tab connected to a loop of stainless steel wire. The wire loop is threaded by hand around the anaesthetized young oyster's adductor muscle, which holds the shell closed. When pulled, the wire acts like a noose, slicing the muscle. Tug the tab and the oyster falls open. The pull-tab oysters, however, are not yet economically viable nor do they seem to have even a potential market amongst oyster eaters, for whom the struggle to reach the fiercely defended flesh inside the shell is apparently an integral part of the gourmet encounter of man and oyster.

2 Oyster Culture

Florus . . . Who can fill the Thames with ships and
merchandise? Rome: only Rome. There is only one
civilisation in the world. Bring Britain into it and she
will grow and prosper: count for something, be alive.
Shut her off into herself, and what is she? An island off
the coast of Gaul, celebrated – for its oysters.
Lawrence Binyon, *Boadicea* (1927)

STRANDLOPERS AND SHELL MIDDENS

Archaeologists have found shell middens, extraordinary
mounds formed by sea shells accumulated over millennia by
early human settlers, along Scandinavian shorelines and down
the west coast of the Americas from the Bering Strait off Alaska
to British Columbia, California, Mexico, Peru and Chile. They
are almost always packed with oyster-shells. In Japan shell middens are horseshoe-shaped and cluster around a central area of
occupation. In Jutland they are elongated and stretch along the
shoreline for 600–700 metres. In Portugal they are as high as
five metres in some places.[1] To the East of Texas, middens cluster along the Gulf Coast all the way to the Florida Keys. The two
oldest-known shell middens in Texas are located near Galveston
Bay and are the remains of Native American campsites from

200,000 Bushels of
Oyster Shells, Hampton, Va.

A postcard showing a large mound of shells outside an oyster shucking plant in Virginia.

3,500 years ago. Some of these shell middens date back to around 40,000 to 12,000 years ago (the Upper Paleolithic), a period in which archaeologists believe that human diets broadened significantly.[2] And shell middens are not just a thing of the past – some hills of shells are still being built outside oyster shucking plants around the world.

Oyster-shell reefs have also formed islands on which humans have built their homes. In Senegal, on the coast south of Dakar, for instance, there is an island called Fadiouth joined to the mainland by a bridge; this is actually an archipelago formed over millions of years by the shells of mangrove oysters, oysters that grow on the extensive tree roots of mangrove trees. The people travel from one island to another and fish for oysters by canoe, paddling across a lagoon paved with oysters, and lined by baobab trees which feed on calcium. The streets are lined with oyster-shells, and in the cemetery, Muslims and

An oyster midden
near Florida, 1915.
The ancient oyster
beds have formed
an island, called
Turtle Mound.

Catholics are buried under startlingly white oyster-shell mounds
in the shade of the mangrove trees.

But what can shell middens tell us about early humans? The fact
that oyster-shells are found in the old Danish *kjokkenmoddings*
shows not only that they were eaten here at an early date but also
that oysters once grew abundantly along the coastline of the
Baltic, which now lacks sufficient salt to support them. Studies
of Danish shell middens show that oysters were harvested
during the extreme spring tides of March and September and
were mostly roasted in the embers of fires to open their shells,
but may also have been dried or smoked. By dating the shells
archaeologists have also discovered that some time between the
Mesolithic and the Neolithic in the Stone Age, the shell middens
change in content from being mostly oysters to being mostly
cockles. This is evidence that there was probably a sea regression
at about this point in the estuaries and bays in which these
people lived, which would have reduced the salt content and
thus the number of oysters. It may also mark a shift from a
hunter/gatherer/fisher culture to a more agricultural one.

Shell middens are found along the southern African coast,
in the open and in caves. They are made up mostly of shellfish

shells, but also contain the bones of terrestrial animals, such as hippopotamus, buffalo, birds, tortoises and snakes, and are believed to be the relics of communities of 'Strandlopers' (beachcombers), in particular the ancestors of a hunter-gatherer tribe called Khoikhoi or Khoekhoe who occupied most of the coastal region from beyond the Orange River to the eastern Cape. Their ancestors farmed and fished along this coast for at least 2,000 years and their descendants still inhabit the region. Johan Albrecht von Mandelslo, who visited the Cape in 1639, called these people Watermen because they lived near the shore, and Leendert Janssen, a survivor from the *Harlem* wrecked in Table Bay in 1647, called them 'Strandlopers'. For some time it was thought that these tribal peoples ate only shellfish, but recent evidence of the shell middens shows that their diet changed from season to season, depending on what meat was available.[3] In the winter oyster flesh, roasted over a fire, supplemented the more scarce hippopotamus or tortoise meat.

OYSTER-BEDS

At some point in human history, men and women turned their minds to cultivating oysters artificially as a way of controlling and increasing their supply. The first people to do so were almost certainly the Chinese; China still produces over 80 per cent of the world's oysters. An ancient Chinese treatise entitled *Fish Breeding* suggests that aquaculture was already in a developed state in 475 BC, but few Chinese records remain.

The most extensive records of early oyster cultivation are those of the Romans. Pliny describes the very first artificial oyster-beds which were laid by a Roman entrepreneur, Sergius Orata, at Baiae just after the Marsic War in 95 BC. Orata seems to have made his money by ambitious water-engineering schemes, for he is also reputed to have invented shower baths. Valerius Maximus described Orata thus:

> unwilling to leave his palate under the control of Neptune's caprice, [he] devised special seas for himself by cutting off the water by means of channels to catch the tide and shutting in various kinds of fish, keeping the molluscs apart so that not even the strongest gale could penetrate. And in this way even lightly-laden tables abounded in a variety of little fishes.[4]

Close to the oyster-beds Orata built a palace where he threw long and decadent parties, feasting through day and night. At every feast thousands of oysters were consumed, only to be politely regurgitated by means of peacock-feather throat ticklers in a room adjoining the banquet. Seneca famously wrote: 'Oysters are not really food, but are relished to bully the sated stomach into further eating.' As oysters became more and more central to the gourmet lifestyle of those living not just in Rome but also in Roman seaside villas, new owners built their houses with salt water tanks of their own. L. Cornelius Lentulus in 50 BC described the menu of a feast:

> Before dinner: sea urchins, raw oysters *ad libitum*, pelorides, spondyli, the fish turdus, asparagus. Next course: fat fowls, oyster patties, pelorides, black and white balani. Next course: spondyli, glycymerides, sea anemones, beccaficos, etc. etc.[5]

Another Roman banquet is described in Becker's 'Gallus':

> Around stood silver dishes containing asparagus, *lactuta*,

radishes and other representations of the garden, in addition to *lacerta*, flavoured both with mint and rue, and with Byzantine *muria*, and dressed snails and oysters, while fresh ones in abundance were handed round. The company expressed their admiration of their host's fanciful invention, and then proceeded to help themselves to what each desired, according to his taste. At the same time slaves carried round in golden goblets the *mulsum*, composed of Hymettian honey and Falernian wines.[6]

The oyster became the caviar or white truffle of the Roman table, sought far and wide or delivered from Orata's artificial beds. Slaves were sent to the sea coast of the Atlantic to gather them. Ever resourceful, the Romans also discovered that ground oyster-shells could be made into ointment to cure wounds, ulcers and chilblains. Oyster-shell powder formed a hard smooth cement for road surfacing or, mixed with figs and pitch, could be used to repair the Roman baths. The oyster had become embedded in the activities of the Roman Empire: in its feasts, its roads and its baths. But it was not until the Empire had reached Britain that, around AD 78, the first oysters were gathered from the shores of Kent, at Richborough (near Whitstable), and carried back to Rome, packed in sacks of snow, so that the shells were held together, where they created a new passion among Roman gourmets. 'Agrippa', writes Bolitho, 'swept Lucrine oysters off the table, and enthroned the British oysters in their place'.[7] British oysters had become the 'new black' in Rome.

Hector Bolitho claims that 'when Rome shivered and became dust, other civilizations took the oyster to their heart and loved it and ate it. And as the art of cooking moved from the crude fire in the open to the refined science of the kitchen, the oyster fired the imagination of cooks and gourmets, until oyster eating could almost be looked upon as a mark of civilization.'[8] Since the Roman and Chinese established their oyster-beds, oyster cultivation has evolved, like the oyster, in scores of different ways, oyster farmers adapting to the conditions of local estuaries and experimenting with local materials to use as cultch. By the beginning of the twentieth century, oyster cultivation was firmly established around the shorelines of the world. An entry in an encyclopaedia for 1911 reads: 'Oysters are more valuable than any other single product of the fisheries, and in at least twenty-five countries are an important factor in the food-supply. The approximate value of the world's oyster crop approaches £4,000,000 annually, representing over 30,000,000 bushels, or nearly 10 billion oysters. Not less than 150,000 persons are engaged in the industry, and the total number dependent thereon is fully half a million. The following table shows in general terms the yearly oyster product of the world.'

Country	Bushels	Value
United States	26,853,760	£2,533,481
Canada	134,140	£43,405
Great Britain and Ireland	113,700	£154,722
France	3,260,190	£716,778
Holland	100,000	£84,400
Italy	68,750	£44,000
Other European countries	29,930	£40,250
Asia, Africa and Oceania	275,000	£111,400
Total	30,835,470	£3,728,436

In 1911 the United States was the biggest global producer of oysters, followed by France and then by 'Asia, Africa and

The Whitstable Oyster Fleet (Dredging).

No. 73641.

Oceania'. Now China and Japan dominate the world's oyster production, with 80 per cent of the total produce.

Methods of oyster cultivation have evolved from country to country. In Japan, oyster culture began centuries ago as an off-shoot of the Japanese or Manila clam industry, particularly around Hiroshima on the northern shore of the Seto inland sea. Clams were grown in shallow-water enclosures surrounded by short fences of interlaced bamboo stalks, called *shibi*. The leaves and stems of the *shibi* collected the larvae of Pacific oysters and the Japanese oyster fishermen soon realized that oysters would yield greater profits than the clams. By the early twentieth century Japanese oyster farmers had adopted hanging-culture techniques that continue today: oyster farmers suspend lengths of rope threaded with clam shells from bamboo rafts floating in the shallows of bays and inlets. Hiroshima still produces 60 per

Postcard showing the Whitstable oyster fleet on a calm morning in the 1930s.

1. Boats going out.　　2. Dredge.　　3. Oyster Bags.　　4. Dredging.　　5. Landing Oysters.

cent of Japan's total production of oysters and has a popular annual oyster festival in February.

In France the great oyster territories are on Brittany's Atlantic coast, which has the bays, coves and estuaries needed for successful cultivation. Most come from Locmariaquer in Morbihan. In 1581 the essayist Michel de Montaigne visited Bordeaux on parliamentary business and recorded:

> They brought us oysters in baskets. They are so agreeable, and of so high an order of taste, that it is like smelling violets to eat them; moreover they are so healthy, a valet gobbled up more than a hundred without any disturbance.[9]

When oyster production went into decline in Europe in the 1850s due to over-consumption, Monsieur Jean Jacques Marie Cyprien Victor Coste, Professor of Embryology at the Collège de France, was employed by the French government to investigate new methods of production. His research began with a journey around the coasts of France and Italy and a journey back

Oyster cultivation in the 19th century at Lago del Fusaro, a coastal lagoon near Naples.

A 'faggot' or bunch of sticks on which oyster spat grow. These are either suspended or anchored in shallow lagoons.

in time to discover the history of Italian and Roman oyster-farming methods. Near Naples he found methods of oyster farming that had been in use since Roman times. In the Lake of Fusaro, a shallow lagoon lying between Lake Lucrino and Cape Miseno, he discovered two methods being practised for farming oysters that had been depicted centuries before on Roman vases. In the first, oyster farmers built mounds of stones on the shore, which were encircled by stakes of wood driven into the sea-bed to keep off predators. In the second method, oyster farmers suspended faggots on ropes strung between stakes in the lagoon.

In 1855 Coste published his findings in *Voyage d'exploration sur le littoral de la France et de l'Italie*, recommending that these techniques be adopted in the French oyster-beds under Government supervision. Ambitious for the French oyster industry and concerned about its decline, Coste wrote a report in February 1858 addressed directly to Napoleon III asking for 6–8,000 francs to experiment in restocking with oysters the Bay of Brieuc on the north coast of Brittany. He proposed growing oysters using the suspended faggot method, much greater regulation of the dredging of the oyster-beds, and a careful mapping and surveillance of the oyster growing areas of the coast. He claimed that if his proposals were adopted the coast of France would become one long chain of oyster-beds.

Napoleon III had imperial ambitions for himself and for France and he looked to the Roman Empire for his inspiration. In 1853 he had appointed Baron Georges Eugène Haussmann to rebuild Paris. By the time Napoleon received Victor Coste's letter outlining his ambitions for the French oyster industry, Haussmann was busy laying arterial road systems, widening

Oyster platforms
in 19th-century
France.

streets, designing new water supplies and sewer systems, and building new bridges, public buildings and parks. The emperor granted Coste the money he asked for his oyster experiment in Brieuc, for he believed in investing in economic enterprises. If European oyster production was in decline, the French would find ways of reinvigorating it.[10] An imperial reputation was at stake.

The experiment in Brieuc was a success, Coste reported a few years later, for there had been a rich harvest of spat: 20,000 young oysters had grown on a single submerged faggot. Coste recommended the immediate restocking of the French coastline along the principles he had developed in Brieuc: a French oyster empire stretching around the colonial territories from Algeria to Corsica as well as along the Mediterranean and Atlantic coasts. The farms would be divided into lots granted to only the most energetic seamen. Oyster farming flourished in Arcachon, south of Bordeaux, and in the Gulf of Morbihan on the Atlantic coast of Brittany, and, certainly by the end of the nineteenth century, France held her own as one of the world's leading oyster producers.

During the nineteenth century oyster industries in America flourished along the north-west coast and in Louisiana and

around Chesapeake Bay, where oyster canning also developed into a major industry in the second half of the century.

The anonymous author of *Lucullus; or, Palatable Essays*, wrote: 'An oyster bed is a pleasure – an El Dorado – a mine of wealth, in fact, which fills the owner's pockets with gold and affords to the million untold gastronomical enjoyment and healthy food'.[11] But by the time this book was published in 1878, oyster production around the world was in decline and no efforts by naturalists with imperial ambitions could stop that decline. Sewage pollution in European waters resulted in a series of large-scale and widely publicized food poisonings in the early twentieth century, after which trade in home-grown oysters and imports fell by 50 per cent. Flat oysters (*Ostrea* species; those that spawn inside their shells) had been decimated by disease and pollution around European, Asian and American shorelines. In the twentieth

These colourfully labelled oyster tins from the USA, mostly dating from the 1890s to the 1930s, are now collectors' items. Seafood packers near the Chesapeake Bay in Maryland filled the tins with raw oysters then shipped them around the world.

century, however, oyster farmers turned to the Pacific oyster
(*Crassostrea* species; those that spawn outside their shells) as an
attempt to restock oyster-farms. After the Second World War,
European oyster farmers found ways of breeding these oysters in
hatcheries. By controlling the water temperature, oyster breed-
ers could induce *Crassostrea* to spawn in any month of the year
and then the spat could be sold to oyster farmers in less warm
climates who could then re-lay the oysters on the foreshore.

One such story of experiment and investment is told by
Richard Pinney, oyster grower of Orford, who came to Suffolk
from London in the 1940s. Sailing his small boat around the
Suffolk coast in 'search of safety and rest' in the last days of the
Second World War, he found Orford, 'bomb-scarred and down
at heel', where he ate fried oysters and bacon at the Trust House.
Having bought a derelict cottage by the side of Butley Creek,
where he could moor his boat, he turned his mind to ways of

A drill-dredge in position for work.

making a living. Ten years or so later, having tried his hand at fishing, fish smoking and the production of rush matting, he determined 'to restore Orford's reputation for oysters'.[12] First he ordered in 20,000 young flat oyster spat from Brittany, which arrived at Victoria Station and which he shipped back to Orford in his Land Rover, laying them on prepared beds in Butley Creek. At the same time he began negotiations with Portuguese oyster growers, finally making a deal with the shipping line to take 120 tons of *Crassostrea* spat. In return they would sail the ship round from Lisbon to Setebul to load the spat to avoid having to drive them across land.

But Pinney's entrepreneurship was dogged by bad luck. The young Portuguese oysters, contained in baskets on deck, were sailed into the British port as a dock strike began. Pinney knew his oysters' lives were at stake:

I took the train up to London in a very sombre mood. I went straight from Liverpool Street Station to the Guildhall Library, where I checked some lines from Shakespeare's Julius Caesar which had come into my mind, and I composed a telegram to our MP, Colonel

(later Sir) Harwood Harrison. It said . . . *Three million lives at stake in London docks stop blame Government's handling of labour troubles stop quote I tell you that which you your-selves do know would I could put a tongue in every wound end quote.*

When this strategy didn't work, Pinney went to his solicitors, the RSPCA and finally the Press. His marooned young oysters made headline news and as a result the dockers volunteered to break their strike to save the oysters, offering to give their earnings to charity. Pinney's rescued and now famous oysters were soon ashore and being transported east to the Orford estuary. There had been hidden benefits, Pinnney realized: 'Orford as an oyster centre, after all this publicity, was once again well on the map'.[13] However, his bad luck returned a few years later: the winter of 1962–3 was severe and the ice in the river suffocated almost all of his oysters, both flat and Pacific. By this point, however, the first generation of transmigrated oysters from Portugal who had broken the London dockers' strike had all been eaten. It was their descendants who died in the ice.

Picking oysters today, from the Pacific oyster beds in the US.

Although Pinney restocked his beds with Pacific oysters after the losses of the 1962 winter, he decided to try another experiment in the early 1970s with a new Pacific oyster, the *Crassostrea gigas*, which had recently arrived from Japan; it grew to adulthood more quickly and showed resistance to cold water. It had been imported as spat and cultivated in America since the 1920s.[14] The Japanese oysters flourished in the waters of the creek but, because the oysters wouldn't spawn in his own cold waters, Pinney had to buy and import new spat every year. In an attempt to avoid having to pay out for annual imports of spat, he began to design and plan his own hatchery, building two pits alongside the river which looked like small swimming baths filled by sea water warmed by electricity. Then he began to experiment with producing algae, and with altering water temperatures and salinity. He recalls watching the spat he had hatched under a microscope:

One of us would be peering in and they would be peering out, confronting us, eyeball to magnified eyeball, along the

barrel of the microscope. At least, that was how it seemed.
As well as eyes, they grew 'feet'. It was as if they were
preparing to escape, to spy out the land, and hoof it![15]

The hatchery experiment, however, proved to be more trouble-
some, labour-intensive and expensive than it was worth.
Eventually the Pinneys decided to continue to buy their spat
from dedicated hatcheries. Oyster labour was, by the 1970s,
generally divided across Europe and Asia between those who
worked in hatcheries and those who relaid the imported spat
in oyster-beds.

Pinney's story of oyster cultivation is one of continual evolution and adaptation, a story that covers a period of only 20 or
30 years, but during which the oyster farmer had to make
changes to his stock, try out new techniques, invest in spat and
deal with decimations to his stock caused by natural disasters
such as cold winters, and human difficulties such as dock strikes.
Though oyster industries have been industrialized to some
extent over the last hundred years and have had to respond to

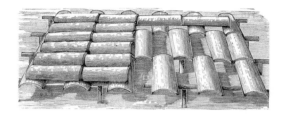

Ways of setting tiles for oyster-growing in France.

new health and safety and food production regulations, a large number of the finest oysters produced on the shores and bays of Europe, Japan, China and America, whether grown suspended from bamboo rafts or on tiles or on muddy estuary beds, are grown in small-scale oyster-farms run by oyster farmers such as Richard Pinney using techniques that – in principle at least – are not dissimilar to those of Sergius Orata.

3 The Rise and Fall of the Oyster

In the first century AD, the Spanish-born Roman poet Martial wrote an epigram addressed to his patron, Ponticus, complaining about the poorer food that his patron served to his lower status guests at his banquets. Ponticus reserved his Lucrine oysters for himself and his most important guests; there were to be no oysters for the poet:

> Now I get a proper invitation to dinner since my days as a paid entertainer are past, why am I given a different dinner from you? You feed on big fat oysters from the Lucrine lagoon; I'm left sucking mussel shells and split lips. You get the choicest mushrooms, I get fungus pigs won't touch. You toy with turbot; I'm down there with the catfish. You stuff yourself with fine roast peacock, its rump indecently plump; laid out on my plate is the kitchen canary's corpse – found dead of old age in its cage. Why don't we dine together, Ponticus, when I come to dinner with you? No longer being hired to come could be a step up the social ladder – if we supped the same.[1]

The oyster has been by turns the food of the rich, the food of the poor and the food the bohemian epicure at different times in human history. For Ponticus, oysters transported to

THE OYSTER STALL.
"Penny a lot, Oysters! Penny a lot!"

A London oyster stall in 1864.

Rome from the Lucrine lagoon were expensive and in short supply, so to be able to serve them at all was a mark of his social standing and his wealth. However, because the early Japanese and Chinese learned to smoke and dry their farmed oysters, they could be added to much more ordinary dishes far inland, away from the sea. Smoked and dried oysters were ubiquitous and easily available in Asia; serving them to guests was not therefore a mark of social standing as serving raw oysters was for the Romans. In other early cultures oysters were a subsistence food: when other food supplies were low they would be harvested straight from the rocks and cooked on open fires on the beach. They had no price. For these people oysters were a fall-back food, not a delicacy.

As techniques of oyster cultivation developed hundreds of years later in the nineteenth century, and the expanding railway network made it possible to transport large numbers of oysters from the sea-beds straight into the rapidly expanding cities, market prices declined sufficiently for oysters to become a subsistence food for the urban poor. For several decades cheap oysters flooded the food markets of Europe. When excessive farming, over-consumption, pollution and the spread of oyster diseases inevitably depleted the oyster supplies of Europe in the late nineteenth century, prices rose steeply.

But factors other than availability and efficiency of transport and refrigeration have affected the oyster's oscillations of status. Changing fashions in food consumption and taste have also played a part. Who eats oysters and where and when? On the street at an oyster stall at midnight, in an oyster tavern cellar for breakfast with friends, in a private inner room as part of an elaborate seduction ritual, or at a banquet laid out with a 100 cut-glass goblets and fine silver? What has it meant to eat oysters? And what have they meant to men and women as *food* at different times in history and in different countries?

When the Romans left Britain around AD 400, the oyster lost its status as a delicacy. For several centuries they were rarely eaten, but by the early eighth century they had returned to favour. In the Old English *Exeter Book* first made public in 1072 by Leofric, first bishop of Exeter, Riddle no. 77 is an oyster:

The deep sea suckled me, the waves sounded over me; waves were my coverlet as I rested on my bed. I have no feet and frequently open my mouth to the flood. Sooner or later some man will consume me, who cares nothing for my shell. With the point of his knife he will pierce me through, ripping the skin away from my side, and straight away eat me uncooked as I am.

Before the Norman Conquest in the eleventh century, the old Roman practice of transporting shellfish inland had been revived, and by the 1400s the oyster was a popular food for rich and poor alike, transported inland in barrels of sea water and usually cooked in its own juices with ale and pepper. An English recipe dated around 1390 suggests that oysters were also being cooked elaborately for the banquets of the rich, for it instructs cooks to 'shell oysters and simmer them in wine and their own broth, strain the broth through a cloth, take blanched almonds, grind them and mix with the same broth and anoint with flour of rice and put the oysters therein, and cast in powder of ginger, sugar and mace'.[2]

By the time that oysters reappeared in British accounts of banquets in the sixteenth and seventeenth centuries, these feasts had acquired a distinctively English character, hearty and meaty, and accompanied by ale, quite unlike the dainty assemblies of morsels of raw seafood, snails and honeyed wine that characterized late Roman feasts. Henry Machin, for instance, 'a citizen and Merchant Taylor of London', describes a *breakfast* oyster feast he consumed in 1557:

On the 30th July, 1557, himself, Master Dave Gyttons, Master Meynard, and Master Drapter, and Master Smyth, Master Caldwella and Master Asse and Gybes, and Master

Dirck Hals, *A Party at Table*, 1625, oil on wood.

opposite:
Oyster-feasting in eighteenth-century France: Jean-François de Troy, *Le Déjeuner d'huîtres*, 1735, oil on canvas.

Fackington, and many more did ett alff a bushell of owsters in Anchur-lane, at Master Smyth and Gyttons' seller, a-pone hoghedes, and candyl lyght, and onyons, and red alle, and claret alle, and muskadylle fre cope, at viii in the mornying.[3]

After oysters, muscatel, red ale and claret ale at eight o'clock in the morning it is difficult to imagine what work these merchants would have been able to undertake, but it seems that the consumption of oysters in a cellar by candlelight was an opportunity for lively conversation and perhaps some business. It was a men-only occasion and this is a common pattern of oyster feasts from as early as Roman times. Since Anchor Lane

probably refers to Blue Anchor Lane (now Keeton's Road) in Bermondsey, only a short distance from the docks at Wapping by the Thames, the oysters that Merchant Machin and his friends consumed are likely to have been only recently delivered to the fish markets along the river. These men were also eating oysters in the month of July, for the practice of avoiding eating oysters in the 'r'-less summer months seems to have begun around this time for health reasons and because spawning oyster meat is poor. In 1599 Samuel Butler wrote in *Dyet's Dry Dinner*: 'it is unseasonable and unwholesome in all months that have not an R in their name to eat oysters'.

In the sixteenth and seventeenth centuries, oysters were often eaten informally in oyster taverns, or ordered from oyster stalls in small barrels, each holding four dozen oysters, to be eaten straight from the barrel. The diarist and writer Samuel Pepys mentions oysters 68 times in his diary – they are the most frequently mentioned seafood, often eaten for breakfast and accompanied by wine:

> [21 May 1660] So into my naked bed and slept till 9 o'clock, and then John Goods waked me, [by] and by the captain's boy brought me four barrels of Mallows oysters . . .
>
> [6 November 1661] Going forth this morning I met Mr Davenport and a friend of his, . . . and I did give them in good wine, and anchovies, and pickled oysters, and took them to the Sun in Fish Street, there did give them a barrel of good ones, and a great deal of wine . . .
>
> [4 December 1665] So late by water home, taking a barrel of oysters with me, and at Greenwich went and sat with Madam Penington . . .

Pepys' descriptions give us a sense of oysters being both a delicacy and what we might call a 'fast food'. Small oysters were cheap enough to buy by the barrel on the way home from visiting friends or the pub. They were not a mark of social status or of wealth but were food for friends and social gatherings, to be eaten in taverns, or in one's own room, or in the street. They were the food of street life and the food of intimate conversation. Paintings of feasts in Holland in the seventeenth century show groups of men and women sitting around tables in richly furnished rooms eating oysters, paintings in which the atmosphere is convivial and relaxed, not elaborately formal. They eat oysters with their fingers and they are all rapt in conversation. When the oyster is shown in yet more intimate situations in these Dutch genre paintings, being passed to a (usually seated) woman by a (usually standing) man, the sense of overheard and impassioned conversation is strong.

However, when they were consumed as part of a more formal feast or banquet in the same period, cooked oysters seem to be the distinguishing line between the upper and lower tables, as the following record of an East India Company feast (20 January 1623) indicates. The upper table had 'rost mutton with oysters' in the first course, 'boyled oysters' in the second course, and then 'oyster pie' and 'picked oysters'. Those sitting at the lower tables were served raw oysters or no oysters at all. Oysters raised their value if they were cooked elaborately, if they were shipped some distance or if they were prized flat oysters from a particular area such as Whitstable. They held an almost mythical status among the high society of seventeenth-century Europe. In 1671 the Prince of Condé's steward fell on his sword after a basket of oysters arrived late for his master's lunch with Louis XIV.

In *Exotic Brew: The Art of Living in the Age of the Enlightenment*, the food historian Piero Camporesi plots the part that oysters

Selling oysters in London, 1804.

played in the changing cuisine of the eighteenth century in Europe, particularly Britain and France. For Camporesi they are the emblematic food of the Enlightenment with their succulent, light, taut and white flesh, 'an expression of the *Lebensgefuhl* of the fledgling century, its hunger for light, trim and nimble bodies (alert and agile, like the new ideas and spirit) in stark contrast to the previous century's floating, blown-out masses of flesh'.[4] Elsewhere, fashions became markedly leaner and lighter; men's clothes and the outlines of furniture became drawn in and streamlined. 'People were developing a new relationship with food. . . . Taste was transformed, excess and splendour

were condemned as evidence of irrational dissoluteness', and it was in this changing culture that oysters found new power and value on the table of the epicure as white delicate flesh: 'Oysters and truffles seized power, forcing all the strong dishes typical of ancient aristocratic tables into exile.'[5]

This was, Camporesi claims, the end of the reign of the dark meats and the beginning of the 'clattering forward march of raw oysters' at the tables of the fashionable and wealthy:

> [game] had now entered a funereal twilight zone. Potent symbols of feudal conviviality and of barbaric aggression,

these glorious black and bloody meats suffered the affront of having to bow to the soft, bloodless and gelatinous pulp-like flesh of oysters . . . [6]

This was a new way of eating. The eighteenth-century aristocratic table was marked by 'a subtle palette of tastes'. It was also marked by a demand for rare foods procured from the furthest reaches of the empire: birds' nests from the Far East cooked in stock and served with butter, cheese and spice, thrushes claws toasted in the candle flame, bear-paws, heads of woodcocks split open and grilled, tea, coffee, ketchup, sorbets and glacé chocolates.

There were still, of course, thousands of oysters sold on street corners in Paris and England during the eighteenth century as these illustrations of oyster sellers show, but they would have been selling much lower-quality oysters. All these sellers were also likely to have set up their stalls close to the sea and river ports and to the fish markets to which the oyster boats sailed. But by the 1840s all this was to change when the spread of the railways and new developments in oyster cultivation made it possible to transport large numbers of cheap and small oysters, called 'scuttlemouths', selling at two for a penny (the modern equivalent of about 12 pence each), straight into the inland industrial cities. Within a few decades, oysters, until only recently savoured as rare delicacies at the banquets of the rich and fashionable, had become a subsistence food for the urban poor. As early as 1836 Charles Dickens described raw oysters as the food of the poor in Chapter 22 of *The Pickwick Papers*:

'It is a very remarkable circumstance, sir,' said Sam, 'that poverty and oysters always seems to go together.'

'I don't understand you, Sam,' said Mr Pickwick.

'What I mean, sir,' said Sam, 'is, that the poorer a place is, the greater call there seems to be for oysters. Look here, sir; here's an oyster stall to every half-dozen houses – the streets lined vith 'em. Blessed if I don't think that ven a man's very poor, he rushes out of his lodgings, and eats oysters in reg'lar desperation'.

In *London Labour and the London Poor* (1851–62) the journalist and social investigator Henry Mayhew described how fish supplies were now brought to

> every poor man's door, both in the thickly crowded streets where the poor reside – a family at least in a room – in the vicinity of Drury-Lane and of Whitechapel, in Westminster, Bethnal-green and St Giles's, and through the long miles of the suburbs. For all low-priced fish the poor are the costermongers' best customers, and a fish diet seems to be becoming almost as common among the ill-paid classes of London, as is a potato diet among the peasants of Ireland.[7]

Mayhew estimates that nearly 500 million oysters and more than 1,000 million herrings passed through Billingsgate in a year, which he says are 'based on facts . . . furnished me by the most eminent of Billingsgate salesmen'. If these statistics are accurate this would mean that the average consumption was around 185 oysters a year per man, woman and child, which seems implausibly high but which still gives us some idea of the increase in oyster consumption brought about by the dramatic fall in prices. Most were scuttlemouths, but some were of a higher quality selling at between 9 and 16 shillings a bushel

(£29–£58 today);[8] the expensive Milton oysters were not easily available from costermonger stalls.

Mayhew also vividly describes the oyster boats selling oysters direct from their boats moored close together at Billingsgate:

> The costermongers have nicknamed the long row of oyster boats moored close alongside the wharf 'Oyster-Street'. On looking down the line of tangled ropes and masts, it seems as though the little boats would sink with the crowds of men and women thronged together on their decks. It is as busy a scene as one can well behold. Each boat has its black sign-board and salesman in his white apron walking up and down 'his shop' . . . These holds are filled with oysters – a grey mass of shell and sand – on which is a bushel measure well piled up in the centre.[9]

Although oysters were still generally avoided during the summer months, it remained customary to eat oysters in London on St James's Day on 25 July. St James is the patron saint of Spain, and his sign is the scallop shell, carried by pilgrims making their way to his shrine in Santiago de Compostela. The illustration on page 68 from the *London Illustrated News* shows how by the nineteenth century many oysters, particularly on oyster day in London, would have been eaten on the street at the oyster stalls themselves. Towards the back of the picture you can see two small children directing the attention of passers-by to a pile of shells they have made up against a lamp-post. Street-children collected oyster-shells from taverns and fish-shops and made small shrines or grottos for St James as a way of begging for money.

In the 1850s Mayhew interviewed an aging oyster seller about her customers. Her reply tells us a great deal about the

Welsh oyster women from Llangwm in Pembrokeshire in the late 19th century. They were good business-women and known to be particularly hardy, walking some 30 miles to Carmarthen to sell their oysters once a week and walking home the next day with their profits.

range of people from different social groups who consumed oysters in the second half of the nineteenth century and show that social divisions were marked in some ways by etiquette about whether oysters could be eaten inside or outside. Clearly the 'poor parsons down on their luck' regarded buying oysters from a costermonger's stall as something to hide, a sign of their poverty. But oysters themselves, eaten as the first course of a banquet or dinner party, would have been a sign of wealth; richer

'The First Day of Oysters: A London Street Scene' in the 1860s, from the *London Illustrated News*. Note the children at the back of the picture building an oyster 'grotto' or shrine to St James, for which they are collecting money.

Oyster seller, engraving by an unnamed artist, 1830.

clients would send servants to the oyster stall to bring back oysters to be eaten in this way. So the genteel poor might have been remembering finer times in their illicit consumption of oysters at the oyster stalls. Interestingly, the oyster seller observed that the 'vulgar poor' were revolted by the idea of eating oysters. So an appreciation of oysters – at least for this oyster seller – remained a way of distinguishing between the genteel and the vulgar poor:

> As to my customers, sir, she said, why, indeed, they're all sorts. It's not a very few times that gentlemen (I call them

so because they're mostly so civil) will stop – just as it's getting darkish, perhaps – and look about them, and then come to me and say very quick: 'Two penn'orth for a whet'. Ah! Some of 'em will look, may be, like poor parsons down upon their luck, and swallow their oysters as if they was taking poison in a hurry.

I many a time think that two penn'orth [54 pence in today's terms] is a poor man's dinner. It's the same often – but only half as often, or not half – with a poor lady, with a veil that once was black, over a bonnet to match, and shivering through her shawl. She'll have the same. About two penn'orth. My son says, it's because that's the price of a glass of gin, and some persons buy oysters instead – but that's only his joke, sir. It's not the vulgar poor that's our chief customers. There's many of them won't touch oysters, and I've heard some of them say: 'The sight of 'em makes me sick; it's like eating snails.' The poor girls that walk the streets often buy; some are brazen and vulgar, and often the finest dressed are the vulgarest . . . One of them always says she must keep at least a penny for gin after her oysters.

My heartiest customers, that I serve with the most pleasure, are working people, on a Saturday night. One couple – I think the wife always goes to meet her husband on a Saturday night – has two, or three, or four penn'orth, as happens, and it's pleasant to hear them say, 'Won't you have another John?' or, 'Do have one or two more, Mary Anne.' I've served them that way two or three years.

I send out a good many oysters, opened for people's suppers, and sometimes for supper parties – at least, I

Richard Caton Woodville, *Politics in an Oyster House*, 1848, oil on canvas.

suppose, for there's five or six dozen often ordered. The maid-servants come for them then, and I give them two or three for themselves.[10]

When oysters were cooked in the nineteenth century they were often combined with other exotic foods, marking new French influences in food prevailing since the end of the Napoleonic Wars. For instance, *The Oyster: Where, How, and When to Find, Breed, Cook and Eat It*, published anonymously in

1861, lists recipes for Fried Oyster, Oyster Soup, Cabbage with Oysters and Fried Larks and Fried Hind Legs of Frogs with Oysters. In the second edition, published in 1863, the author lists places to buy and eat oysters in London and these include Rule's oyster shop in Maiden Lane, Scott's in Coventry Street, Wilton's in Great Ryder Street, and Sweeting's beyond St Paul's. Wilton's, founded in 1742, catered for the aristocracy and royalty and supplied Whitstable oysters to the court from the time of George III to George VI (reigned 1936–52). Clearly this anonymous writer's oyster directions were for those with money to spend.

In America oysters had been harvested and eaten by Native Americans who lived along the coasts and, when dried or smoked, used to trade with inland tribes. When the early colonists came to America they often described with admiration the abundant oyster-beds along the east coast as part of their rhetoric of describing the new world as the land of riches: the land of milk, honey and . . . oysters. In 1607, for instance, a group of settlers landed at Cape Henry, which was later to become part of the State of Virginia. One of the settlers, George Percy, described coming upon a tribe of Native Americans: 'they had made a great fire, and had been newly roasting oysters. When they perceived our coming they fled away to the mountains and left many of the oysters in the fire. We ate some of the oysters, which were very large and delicate in taste'.[11] But in 1680 settlers in Maryland complained to British authorities that their provisions were in such short supply that 'it was necessary for them, in order to keep from starvation, to eat the oysters taken from along their shores'.[12] From such accounts it seems that by this latter point of settlement, oysters were seen as a subsistence food associated with the eating customs of the natives, not a delicacy for 'civilized' settlers.

In the eighteenth century Captain Cook marvelled at the size and abundance of oysters he found along the coasts of Australia and New Zealand and sent his men to stock up the boat each time they landed on an oyster-rich shore or creek. He watched the natives collecting oysters in Botany Bay in May 1770 from his boat:

On the sand and Mud banks are Oysters, Muscles, Cockles, etc., which I believe are the Chief support of the inhabitants, who go into Shoald Water with their little Canoes and peck them out of the sand and Mud with their hands, and sometimes roast and Eat them in the Canoe, having often a fire for that purpose, as I suppose, for I know no other it can be for.[13]

But if oysters were a subsistence food, gathered and dried by Cook's men and, on some parts of the journey, perhaps the only food they lived on, they were nonetheless still regarded as a delicacy provided abundantly by these paradisiacal shores.

By the nineteenth century oysters had become ubiquitous in America too, and like England, the food of both rich and poor, formal food of the great banquet and informal food of the street. In 1842 Charles Dickens visited America for the first time and befriended the oyster-lover Cornelius Felton, Professor of Greek at Harvard. The two went 'roistering and oystering in New York', eating their oysters from stalls and talking to local oyster sellers. Later Dickens would correspond with Felton, writing letters that were full of oyster comedy, including this extract in which he pondered over what oyster openers did in New York in the summer months when oysters were out of season:

Do they commit suicide in despair, or wrench open tight drawers and cupboards and hermetically sealed bottles –

'Bernstein's Fish Grotto', a San Francisco oyster shop, was established in 1912.

for practice? Perhaps they are dentists out of the oyster season. Who knows.[14]

Felton accompanied Dickens to a huge reception that the people of New York had organized for Dickens's visit, which was attended by 3,000 people and at which 50,000 oysters were served to both male and female guests. It seems that in America oyster eating had become democratized at such large public occasions far earlier than it would be in Britain. There is no evidence that the mayor of New York kept the best oysters for the most important guests, for he had ordered more than a dozen oysters per guest.

In Britain, city oyster feasts remained exclusive events until the early twentieth century, and the guest lists from the early nineteenth century to the early twentieth mirror in interesting ways the gradual opening up of the franchise. As the status of citizens changed – and perhaps because votes were now to be won – so city oyster feasts would cater to much larger numbers of guests each year. In 'Civic Ritual and the Colchester Oyster Feast',[15] the historian David Cannadine shows how the oyster festival held in Colchester was democratized gradually during the nineteenth and twentieth centuries. Between 1800 and 1870 the oyster feast took the form of a small private feast held by the wealthier Tory and Anglican members of the corporation. By 1880, when the more democratic city council established a grammar school and became increasingly central to the life of the city, it turned the oyster feast into a grand, public pageant open to all the men in the city (the franchise had been extended to include all men in 1867). A new town hall was built in 1897, in part to house the feast. It is striking how closely oyster feast enfranchisement mirrors political enfranchisement for women were allowed to attend the oyster feast only after 1914; the right to vote was granted to women only over the age of 30 in 1918 and to all women in 1928.

Given Cannadine's thesis about the Colchester oyster feast being a ritual around which civic responsibility and pride were modelled, a sonnet to the oyster written for the Diamond Jubilee Toast list in 1897 (when the feast was still a men-only affair) shows the oyster anthropomorphized as a model of civic virtues, the spirit of the feast itself – and quite definitely a masculinized set of values:

> To public men – and private men as well –
> The Moral of the Feast these verses tell.
> In spite of foes, which everywhere abound,
> The cool impassive Oyster keeps his ground:
> Tenacious, firm, in temper unexcelled,
> His mouth kept shut, unless he is compelled,
> And then imparting only what he should,
> Not for his own, but for the public good,
> All sweet, agreeable, in perfect taste,
> With nought superfluous to vex – or waste;
> Unselfishly relinquishing his ease,
> His only object seems to be to please.[16]

This sonnet celebrating the oyster as a civically minded creature reverses the range of poetic anthropomorphisms the oyster has assumed over hundreds of years. It is much more usually associated with stupidity or silence or inertia and almost always with a kind of solipsistic individualism, as Eleanor Clark writes: 'Though the oyster spawn and teem, it is always oyster – singular that is used in culture: silent as an oyster, alone as an oyster . . . '[17] Dickens, for instance, described Scrooge in *A Christmas Carol* as 'secret, and self-contained, and solitary as an oyster'. But for the civic feast for which this oyster poem was written, the poet enlisted the oyster in the rhetoric of town pride and civic responsibility. Oyster anthropomorphisms it seems, like the oyster itself, can turn every which way.

But if the oyster at Colchester was civic food, marking respectability and responsibility, it was elsewhere the food of the street and of the outsider, the *flâneur*, the bohemian. In the second half of the nineteenth century the proliferating taverns and inns serving oysters were the haunt of artists and writers. As they had been for Samuel Pepys some 300 years earlier, eating oysters at midnight or first thing in the morning was an essential part of the pleasures of bohemian living, food eaten with other *bon-viveurs* amongst the urban poor, an underground pleasure taken on the edges of the day. The journalist George Augustus Sala, bohemian *par excellence*, documented the street life of London in *Twice Round the Clock; or, the Hours of the Day and Night in London* (1859) location by location. He casts himself as the *flâneur*, walking the streets of London for inspiration, the urban voyeur. The pleasures of the oyster are reserved for midnight:

> But we have come to the complexion of midnight and the hour must be described. It is fraught with meaning for London. You know that in poetical parlance midnight is the time when graveyards yawn . . . and graves give up their dead. And there be other grave-yards in London town – yards where no tombstones of brick-vaults are – that at midnight yawn and send forth ghosts to haunt the city. A new life begins for London at midnight. Strange shapes appear of men and women who have lain a-bed all the day and evening, or have remained torpid in holes and corners.

They come out arrayed in strange and fantastic garments, and in glaringly gaslit rooms screech and gabble in wild revelry. The street corners are beset by night prowlers. Phantoms arrayed in satin and lace flit upon the sight. The devil puts a diamond ring upon his taloned finger, sticks a pin in his shirt; and takes his walks abroad . . .[18]

At this point Sala takes a tour of the coffee houses, cafés, restaurants of Haymarket, but his imagined reader or companion refuses all these and demands that only oysters be the order of the night. Sala writes: 'The London oyster-shop, and particularly the Haymarket one, stands, and is a thing apart, among the notabilia of the metropolis.' He contrasts it to the French and American oyster bars. The French oyster bars he rejects for several reasons: they serve oysters with other foods, their oysters are too coppery, they don't serve Cayenne pepper and because they don't eat enough or vigorously enough they have 'nimby-pimby ways'. New York oyster shops, however, are considerably better, he claims:

> During the gay night, brilliant lamps, sometimes covered in fantastic devices, invite you to enter underground temples of oyster-eating. These are called oyster-cellars. Some are low and disreputable enough, and not inpassible to imputations of gouging, bowie-knifing, and knuckle-dusting; but others are really magnificent suites of apartments, decorated with mirrors and chandeliers, and glowing with gilding, mahogany and crimson velvet; and here you may consume oysters as small as periwinkles or as large as cheese-plates, oysters of strange and wondrous flavours – oysters with bizarre and well-nigh unpronounceable names – oysters cooked in ways the

most marvellous and multifarious: stewed, broiled, fried, scalloped, barbecued, toasted, grilled and made hot in silver chafing dishes . . .

Yet for all the splendour and rarity of the cooking, and the variety of the oysters, I will abide by the Haymarket oyster-shop, rude, simple, primitive as it is, with its peaceful concourses of customers taking perpendicular refreshment at the counter . . . calling cheerfully for crusty bread and pats of butter; and tossing off foaming pints of brownest stout . . .[19]

The decline in oyster production across Europe in the late nineteenth century and the early twentieth changed patterns of oyster consumption once again. During the First World War the slaughter of millions of the young men of Europe left oyster-beds abandoned around France and Britain. In the 1930s,

Selling oysters to the troops during the First World War, a morale-boosting postcard sent to Britain from France.

'Oyster Bill' with his stall on Blackpool sands in the 1930s.

however, oyster sellers still plied their wares at oyster stalls wheeled on the sands of Blackpool and other seaside towns, a vestige of old England. In Blackpool there were as many as fifteen or sixteen stalls on the beaches in season, many owned by Irishmen who came over for the summer season.

One Blackpool resident commented to the oyster writer Robert Nield: 'Isn't it funny that people have been in all sorts of jobs, selling all sorts of things on stalls, they've done everything, but shellfish has lasted everyone out'.[20] During the Second World War, food rationing and austerity changed attitudes to gourmet foods, but the return of those who had served in occupied France brought new food cultures into Britain. After the war, as ex-servicemen set out to make a living outside the cities

Artists dining on oysters at the London restaurant Wheeler's in 1962. Timothy Behrens, Lucien Freud, Francis Bacon, Frank Auerbach and Michael Andrews, photograph by John Deakin.

and to revive the oyster-beds, oyster production began to pick up slowly again.

In the late 1950s and '60s as post-war austerity waned, interest in foreign food rose dramatically: men and women queued in supermarkets for Italian pastas and French wines and ate in Asian restaurants. Once again oysters became the food of the epicure, the bohemian and the artist. In the photo above Lucien Freud, Francis Bacon and friends eat oysters and drink champagne at Wheeler's in London in 1962. Michael Peppiatt, Bacon's biographer, writes:

Once he had done his morning's work in the studio, Bacon would arrive around noon in Soho, have a few glasses of white wine, then move on for lunch . . . to Wheeler's, his favourite fish restaurant, around the corner in Old Compton Street . . . His guests would often include other artists, writers and intellectuals – as well as some drunken bruisers or East End toughs. Wheeler's became the ultimate club for Bacon, a place where he knew everyone, could sign for meals and cash a cheque.[21]

If the oyster-shell has been used as a way of dating rock strata or early archaeological sites, oyster flesh can be used as a way of marking changing food cultures from the Romans to the present day. If Martial, the Roman poet, was outlawed from the oyster-eating tables of his wealthy patron, these twentieth-century painters were now at the centre of the bohemian oyster feast; they needed no patrons to provide their oysters.

As food, then, oysters have been all things to all people, rising and falling in popularity as prices have been effected by conditions of farming and supply and transport systems. Wherever they are eaten, however, by Pepys at midnight on the street, or by the city banker discussing business over lunch in the early twenty-first century, or by the factory worker at an oyster stall on Blackpool beach, oysters are the food of the transient moment and of the epicure, rich and poor alike.

4 Oysters and Gluttony

Since the Romans the oyster has been associated with gluttony and acts of gluttonous bravado and used for moral homilies about the consequences of greed. In La Fontaine's seventeenth-century fable 'The Rat and the Oyster', a rat 'of weak mind and brain' sets forth to travel the land. On the shoreline he finds an oyster-bed and, spotting an oyster with its shell open, reaches forward to consume the flesh, only to find itself caught in the oyster's tightly closed shell. Fontaine offers several morals: that those who are ignorant of the world 'judge every trivial object to be an astonishing revelation' and that 'the would-be trapper is often trapped'.[1]

The animal oyster eater – whether fox, rat or mouse – in animal fables around the world is almost always portrayed as a warning against greed or stupidity. The animal driven by hunger is blinded to danger. He – and the animal oyster eater is almost *always* he – is impetuous and doesn't stop to think. His body drives him, not his reason. The oyster, seemingly inert and passive, takes its revenge. Buried in such warnings about the dangers of reaching out for seemingly passive and inviting flesh, are surely warnings against sexual invitation and the dangers of following the promptings of the flesh rather than reason.

In 1736 the poet Samuel Bowden was commissioned to write a poem about the skeleton of a mouse caught in an oyster-shell displayed in the local museum. He wrote a moral poem in the tradition of La Fontaine called 'The Mouse and the Oyster: Occasioned by a Mouse Caught in an Oyster Shell'. An anthropomorphized epicurean – and once again male – mouse patrols 'silent mansions' at night in search of food.

In some ill hour, he crept where Oyster lay.
The Fish, commission'd from the watery throng,
With tegument of scaly armour strong,
Lay with expanded mouth – an horrid cell!
What pen the dire catastrophe can tell?
Stretch't on the shore, thus ready for surprise,
With jaws expanded, Nile's dread monster lies.
Th' insatiable thief, now fond of some new dish,
Explores the dark apartment of the fish,
Conscious of bearded touch, the Oyster fell,
And caught the head of caitiff in the shell.

In vain the victim labours to get free.
From durance hard, and dread captivity:
Lock't in the close embrace – dire fate! He lies
In pillory safe – pants, struggles, squeaks and dies.
Instructed thus – let Epicures beware,
Warn'd of their fate – not seek luxurious fare.[2]

In the nineteenth century Dando, a notorious London oyster thief, was the subject of many cartoons, ballads, and a play written in 1838. He was reputed to have been brought before the magistrates several times a month for having refused to settle his bill after overeating in an oyster shop. But although the Dando stories may carry vestiges of a moral, Dando is primarily represented as a kind of folk hero, transgressing the law to

The comic actor Stubby Kaye, a star of the Broadway musical *L'il Abner*, eating oysters in New York in the 1960s.

follow his own singular passions. A kind of oyster-eating pirate living outside the law. Charles Dickens described him in a letter:

> He used to go into oyster shops, without a farthing of money, and stand at the counter eating Natives, until the man who opened them grew pale, cast down his knife, staggered backward, struck his white forehead with his open hand, and cried 'you are Dando!!!'. He has been known to eat twenty dozen at one sitting; and would have eaten forty, if the truth had not flashed upon the shop keeper . . . For these offences he was constantly committed to the House of Correction . . . They buried him in the Prison Yard, and paved his Grave with oyster shells.[3]

One dozen oysters may be a reasonable number to consume in one sitting, but twenty dozen – that's 240 oysters – is heroic. After Dando's death, *Punch* published a delightful poem supposedly written by Dando's spirit from beyond the grave:

> A message from the Spirit-sphere,
> List ye, who linger behind:
> I found not any oysters here,
> Which did at first disturb my mind.[4]

In almost all these stories of excessive *human* consumption of oysters the subjects – like Dando – are men, and there is a note of admiration in the way their stories are told. They have a lust for life, and show no restraint in the pleasures of the flesh. These are the Casanovas of oyster flesh. There is, however, one hazy story of a *woman* oyster eater told in several of the histories of oysters but in different ways. Some say she was a Spanish oyster seller who frequented the bars of Madrid; others that she was Parisian. The details of her identity are vague but the event is the same in all versions: she made a bet with a group of men that she could consume a dozen oysters on each stroke of midnight, interspersed with glasses of champagne. That's 144 oysters and 12 glasses of champagne. She won her bet and passed into history as an oyster-eating heroine of bohemian midnight.

OYSTER WARS, LAWS AND LEGISLATION

To protect oyster supplies from human over-consumption of the Dando kind, governments around the world have had to write oyster laws and oyster acts for three main reasons: to legislate about when oysters can be harvested to prevent over-farming; to prevent disputes breaking out between oyster dredgers from different countries, states or villages about oyster-bed boundaries; and to create legislation to prevent outbreaks of food poisoning. To enforce these laws, oyster superintendents or inspectors of health, or oyster 'police' have been appointed since the early eighteenth century. However, the details of these laws reveal that a good deal more has been at stake than public health and oyster conservation.

In 1715, for instance, the first oyster law was passed in New York, ostensibly to protect the supply of oysters. Its stipulations, however, reveal a great deal about race and the oyster industry in eighteenth-century New York, then a small settlement (covering the area that runs from Wall Street south to the tip of Manhattan) ruled from London as part of British America:

From and under the publication of this act, it shall not be lawful for any person or persons whatever, native free Indians only excepted, from and after the first day of May until the first day of September, annually to gather, rake, take up or bring to the market any oysters whatever, under the penalty of twenty shillings for every offence, to be recovered before any of his Majesty's Justices of the Peace, who are hereby authorised and required to hear, and finally determine the same, one-half thereof to turn to him or them that shall bring the same to effect, and the other half to the poor of the place where the offence shall have been committed. And it shall not be lawful for any negro, Indian, or mulatto slave to sell any oyster in the city of New York, at any time whatsoever, under the penalty of twenty shillings for every offence, to be paid by the master or mistress of such slave or slaves, to be recovered and applied as aforesaid.[5]

The British did not introduce a law determining a closed season for oysters until over 100 years later – during the 1840s, which was a decade of economic depression and widespread famine in England, Scotland and Ireland. Again the overt motive of this legislation may have been to protect oyster supplies from over-farming, but it is clear that the legislation was also about relations and disputes between Britain and France in the years after the end of the Napoleonic Wars. The law of 1843 determined a closed season for oyster fishing and dictated that no boat in the English Channel should carry any dredge or other equipment for catching oysters, but it also stipulated that the fishermen of each nation should not fish within three miles of the coast of the other nation. However, the British government rarely enforced this law as far as British fishermen were concerned.

Despite the existence of laws, policing oyster-beds is almost impossible when the beds are invisible beneath the water. Before the availability of instruments that measured latitude and longitude, the boundaries of oyster and fishing grounds were fixed in relation to natural features on the land as this seventeenth-century Whitstable document reveals:

> The fishing begins East from an oak called Scott's Oak in
> Clowe's Wood upon Rayham Trees, in the Stream so far
> off as Blackbourne's House, a sail's breadth in Shelness
> on Sheppey, and as far West in the same Stream as Scott's
> Oak upon Whitstable Church.[6]

In the nineteenth century the increase in demand for oysters caused ferocious disputes to break out between oyster fishermen of different villages. It was not now enough to claim that a tree in the distance was a marking post between one bed and another.

Oyster boats on the Firth of Forth, Scotland, 1900.

Oyster-dredging on the Firth of Forth in the nineteenth century is a good example of the violence of such disputes over oyster-bed boundaries. Charles Darwin enrolled as a student at the Medical Faculty of Edinburgh in 1825 when he was 16 years old. Developing an interest in the anatomy of sea creatures that would eventually lead to the beginnings of his theory on natural selection, Darwin often sailed out with the oyster men from Newhaven, a village a mile or so along the coast from Leith, Edinburgh's port. The oyster boats were small and carried four men who left at daybreak and rowed and dredged all day, singing fishing shanties to set the pace of their oars. But this was a dangerous occupation in the 1820s, Darwin recorded, for with no demarcations on the sea in the Firth of Forth to mark the end of one bed and the beginning of another, disputes often broke out between the oyster dredgers of Newhaven and those of Prestonpans. There was much at stake: 30 million oysters a year were dredged up from the Firth of Forth. Sometimes a Prestonpans boat would capture a Newhaven boat or vice versa, board it and run it ashore. Curiosity and the opportunity to study rare sea creatures dredged up from the Firth of Forth motivated the young medical student to overcome both his fear of oyster piracy and his severe seasickness.[7]

These disputes on the Firth of Forth continued throughout the century, long after Darwin had left, as oyster demand remained high. In 1870, when some Brightlingsea smacks sailed to the Firth of Forth to dredge for oysters, the Firth fishermen attacked them with boats laden with stones. The Brightlingsea men had to sleep under police protection, armed with hatchets and pokers, and finally a gunboat was dispatched to restore order.

But the most famous dispute over oyster-bed boundaries broke out in Chesapeake Bay in the United States. There had been oyster disputes there for two centuries between the local

Poachers at
Chesapeake Bay
dredging oysters
at night, from
Harper's Weekly,
late 19th century.

fishermen and poachers because of disagreements over titles
between the states of Maryland and Virginia: Virginia owned
part of the Bay, but Maryland owned the entire Potomac River,
and there had been bitter rivalry between the oyster police of the
two states. In 1959 a poacher called Berkeley Muse was killed in
a blaze of gunfire from an oyster patrol boat. After that death
the two states passed an act establishing a joint Potomac River
Fisheries Commission, signed by President Kennedy in 1962,
which created a bi-state commission to govern the river.

In Britain, as oyster production continued to decline, the
government established a Royal Commission on Sea Fisheries
in 1863 with only three members, T. H. Huxley, G. Shaw Lefevre,
and James Caird. This led to the establishment of new laws in
1866 and 1867 through which almost all public regulation of the
oyster fisheries was abolished. A system of private enclosure
was introduced in the hope that more private control would
result in the production of more oysters. When oyster produc-

A Victorian era cartoon after Charles Keane from *Punch*.

UNTIMELY!

Patient (with Limited Income). "OH, DOCTOR, DON'T LET ME SLIP THROUGH YOUR FINGERS THIS TIME——JUST AS OYSTERS ARE GOING TO BE CHEAP AGAIN!"

tion continued to decline, a Select Committee was established in 1876 that found, of course, that over-dredging was still the cause. A witness who reported to the Select Committee described what had happened when a new bed was found on the Whitstable Flats:

> Within 48 hours of that fishery being discovered, I count-
> ed, I think it was, 75 boats upon this one little spot. I went
> there myself; it was quite a narrow limit, about 30 yards
> long and 10 broad, and upon this I dredged. The boats

were jammed together. You went up and down with boats on each side touching.[8]

But during the 1860s the price began to rise. By 1865 the price of natives was between 50 pence and 75 pence per oyster in modern terms and, by 1889, closer to £2 each. Oyster production had collapsed. On 15 October 1867 *The Times* lamented the results of such over fishing:

> From prehistoric man to August, 1864, is a long stretch of time – 'from July to eternity', the Americans are wont to say when they speak of such intervals. And what has been done in that period? Why, all the Oysters in the sea, or at least in our seas, have been eaten up. There are no longer as good fish in the sea as ever came out of it. The Oysters are gone and no wonder . . .
>
> The fact is that a wild Oyster has become pretty well as rare as a wild horse. We are obliged to economise what stock we have got, and breed a supply for ourselves – no easy matter. An Oyster takes three times as long to grow as a sheep. The creature must actually be four years old before he is fit for the table, whereas we can get very good mutton now-a-days in thirteen months . . .
>
> Our fishermen, French and English between them, have cleared the bottom of the sea out . . . It is the old story of the salmon fisheries over again, with this aggravation, – that the Oysters cannot run away from their destroyers, nor be induced to come back again when the persecution is over.

This sense of scandal at human greed and exploitation of natural resources must also have been behind Lewis Carroll's famous poem 'The Walrus and The Carpenter', written for *Alice*

Through the Looking-Glass and published only four years later, in 1871.[9] The young oysters are lured from the sea onto the beach by the charms of the walrus and the carpenter and then eaten by the two gluttonous epicures (once again, both are men):

> 'O Oysters, come and walk with us!'
> The Walrus did beseech.
> 'A pleasant walk, a pleasant talk,
> Along the briny beach:
> We cannot do with more than four,
> To give a hand to each.'
>
> The eldest Oyster looked at him.
> But never a word he said:
> The eldest Oyster winked his eye,
> And shook his heavy head –
> Meaning to say he did not choose
> To leave the oyster-bed.
>
> But four young oysters hurried up,
> All eager for the treat:
> Their coats were brushed, their faces washed,
> Their shoes were clean and neat –
> And this was odd, because, you know,
> They hadn't any feet.

The Walrus lures the oysters not only with charm but with the wit of his conversation: 'The time has come, the Walrus said/ To talk of many things. /Of shoes – and ships – and sealing wax – / And cabbages – and kings – '. When the time comes for the oyster feast the Walrus is contrite, but not contrite enough to abstain from eating the young oysters:

'I weep for you,' the Walrus said.
'I deeply sympathize.'
With sobs and tears he sorted out
Those of the largest size.
Holding his pocket handkerchief
Before his streaming eyes.

'O Oysters,' said the Carpenter.
'You've had a pleasant run!
Shall we be trotting home again?'
But answer came there none –
And that was scarcely odd, because
They'd eaten every one.

John Tenniel, illustration for Lewis Carroll's poem, 'The Walrus and the Carpenter'. In a later version of the poem in operatic form the oysters rise up and take their revenge.

When Alice discusses the poem with Tweedledee and Tweedledum – a mock heroic argument about whether the walrus or the carpenter is the better person – her dilemma concerns having to choose between judging a person in terms of his acts or his intentions. She remembers that the carpenter ate fewer oysters, but the walrus ate his larger share with remorse.[10] How to weigh one against the other?

Interestingly, when Henry Savile Clarke reworked 'The Walrus and the Carpenter' into an operetta in 1886 called *Alice in Wonderland: A Dream Play for Children in Two Acts*, with music composed (appropriately enough) by a composer called Walter Slaughter, Carroll suggested changing the ending so that the oysters could have their revenge. Whilst the Walrus and the Carpenter, engorged from their oyster feast, sleep on the sand, the ghosts of the oysters rise up. The ghost of the second oyster dances a horn-pipe and sings:

> O woeful, weeping Walrus, your tears are all a sham!
> You're greedier for Oysters than children are for jam.
> You like to have an Oyster to give the meal a zest –
> Excuse me, wicked Walrus, for stamping on your chest!
> For stamping on your chest!
> For stamping on your chest!
> For stamping on your chest!
> Excuse me, wicked Walrus, for stamping on your chest!

The oyster uprising brought the audiences to their feet, cheering. This was clearly both a class act and a gastronomic one. The oyster gluttons had received their comeuppance. The enthusiasm of the crowd for the oyster uprising is not surprising, for the 1880s were a decade of marked anti-aristocratic feeling and of organized working-class protest. In 1885 the journalist W. T.

Stead had led a passionate newspaper campaign in the *Pall Mall Gazette* drawing attention to the prostitution of children in London, portraying the aristocratic clients in search of underage virgins as monsters feeding on the daughters of the poor. In 1888 the Bryant & May match-girls came out on strike, supported by radical journalists and suffragettes who called their employment a 'white slave trade' and portrayed their employers as greedy exploiters of the urban poor. There are countless other examples of the demonization of sexual and capitalist greed in the 1880s in political invective, speeches, journalism and in poetry and literature. Carroll saw the opportunity of turning his tale of epicurean greed into a parable of class conflict in which the oysters, though dead, were given a chance to act out the revenge of the repressed.

Greed, then, in relation to oysters is largely relative. In the eighteenth century stories about animal oyster eaters may have been used as warnings about greed, but by the middle of the nineteenth century human oyster gluttons acquired a legendary character coming to represent a flamboyantly lawless epicureanism. By the 1880s, when anti-aristocratic feeling and protestations about the exploitation of the weak by the rich and powerful converged with new ideas about the conservation of natural resources, the oyster glutton of Carroll's operetta was now to be punished by the ghost victims of his greed. By this point the oyster-beds of Europe were perceived to be almost beyond rescue, depleted by over-farming and by greed.

Oyster-eating competitions are still held as the jewels in the crown of oyster festivals around the world. The oyster festival and oyster-eating competition has its roots in the nineteenth-century when the restrictions on oyster selling were lifted at the start of the season on 1 September, and epicures mobbed oyster sellers at their stalls. In truly Dionysiac and carnivalesque

A 1950s Guinness advertisement. Its reference to 'going native' plays on flat oysters or 'natives', which were, of course, produced on Irish shores. It also implies a barbarism about the eating of oysters that echoes, probably unintentionally, the 19th-century association of Irishness and savagery.

opposite:
A 1960s US advertisement for Porsche cars. In its implication that oysters are an acquired taste associated with the aristocracy, this ad contrasts interestingly with the Guinness one.

Are you going Native?

The natives have always been extremely friendly towards Guinness. In fact, Guinness and oysters are inseparable. And there's many a good fish in the sea that will be enjoyed to the full with Guinness.

GUINNESS ALWAYS GOES WITH OYSTERS

spirit, excessive consumption of wine or oysters temporarily replaces the usual restraints and moral imperatives and etiquette about food consumption within daily life. Oyster eating competitors, still largely male, gorge on sweet oyster flesh washed down by wine in marquees or town halls across America, Britain, France, South Africa, China and India. New competitions have emerged recently, however, in which paired (usually

98

■ Not even the most fastidious gourmet was born with a fondness for oysters or the desire for truffles, a fungus which grows wild underground and can be harvested only with the aid of trained dogs and pigs whose noses are peculiarly sensitive to its delicate scent.

Such tastes are acquired by those who seek the ultimate for their palates. No different from those motorists who drive Porsches.

They sampled lesser cars. They wanted superior performance and unique driving pleasure. These tastes led them to the automobile whose qualities have been proven by victories in international road racing and hill climbing competition.

Good things...oysters, truffles, caviar... are always in short supply. Porsche is a good car...the best, some authorities insist.

Only 60 are built each day. Hand assembly is painstaking; Porsche testing procedures are exhaustive.

Driving a Porsche may feel strange, at first...the quickness, the positive steering action, the fast, straight stops. The rear-engine, torsion-bar suspension, four-wheel disc brakes, and smooth, synchromesh gearbox take a little getting used to.

But watch it. Once you get hooked, it's for life! Inevitably, nothing less than the unique Porsche performance will satisfy you. After all, caviar connoisseurs don't go back to tuna fish salad.

Prices start at about $5,100, East Coast P.O.E. See your Porsche dealer or write to the Porsche of America Corporation, 100 Galway Place, Teaneck, N.J. 07666.

PORSCHE

Porsche is an acquired taste

male–female) entrants compete as one partner opens the shells and passes the oyster flesh into the open mouth of his or her blindfolded companion.

In America and Japan, however, food competitions are not relegated to the marquees of annual festivals, but are held all year round, sponsored and regulated by the supposedly 'International' Federation of Competitive Eating. One of its members is Boyd Bulot, a Louisiana self-publicist and professional eating-contest competitor, who travels the world entering hot-dog, burger, matzo ball and oyster-eating competitions. He set a world record at the Acme Oyster House World Oyster Eating Competition in Louisiana in 2003 by swallowing 216 Louisiana oysters in just 10 minutes, beating his main rival, a New Yorker called 'Crazy Legs' Conti, who won the Coveted Belt of Oyster Eating Greatness in 2002. 'And after that I had a seafood platter, French fries and some cheesecake', Bulot told journalists. Whilst such stories may conform to European social stereotypes about American – and indeed Western capitalist – greed, such stereotypes also gloss over age-old cultural contradictions, for whilst Louisiana is the home of the World Oyster Eating Competition, the state of Louisiana continues to be a leading agency in the conservation of oyster reefs.

5 Oyster Flesh: Desire and Abjection

What might have driven prehistoric woman to prise open a barnacle-encrusted oyster-shell and slip its grey, wet flesh into her mouth? Jonathan Swift listed as a proverbial cliché in 'Polite Conversation' (1738) the statement 'He was a bold man that first did eat an oyster', but it is a scenario that has taxed food historians and philosophers in a number of musings on the subject. All such meditations start from the assumption that the first oyster eater was a man. John Gay wrote in *Trivia; or, the Art of Walking the Streets of London* in 1716:

> The man had sure a plate covered o'er
> With brass or steel, that on the rocky shore
> First broke the oozy oyster's pearly coat
> And risked the living morsel down his throat.

And in 1857 the American lawyer and judge James Watson Gerard's first oyster eaters in his satirical *Ostrea; or, the Loves of the Oysters* were not prehistoric hunters but ancient epicurean kings:

> Was't Phut, or Peleg, or Shem, or great Magog?
> Or lively Nimrod, or perhaps his dog?

Or did the royal lips of great Nebu
Chadnozzor first smack over you;
Ere yet, a ruminant, this stately sinner
Was sent, with cows and goats, to pick his dinner?
Or broiled, or roasted, did thy unctuous savour
Perfume the marble halls of old Belshazzar?
Did Pharoah gulp thee, 'ere the sea gulped him?
Or Troglodyte, or Scandinavian grim?
Long, long ago.[1]

When the nineteenth-century popular science writer Louis
Figuier, who wrote several pieces speculating on early human
life, meditated on the psychology of the first oyster eater in *The
Ocean World* (1868), he portrayed prehistoric man as a romantic
outcast, an anti-diluvian *flâneur*:

Once upon a time a man of melancholy mood was walking by the shores of a picturesque estuary, listening to
the monotonous murmur of the sad sea-waves when he
espied a very old and ugly oyster-shell, all coated over
with parasites and sea-weeds. It was so unprepossessing
that he kicked it with his foot, and the animal aston-
ished at receiving such rude treatment on its own
domain, gaped wide with indignation, preparatory to
closing its valves still more tightly. Seeing the beautiful
cream-coloured layers that shone within the shelly covering, and fancying that the interior of the shell itself
must be beautiful, he lifted up the aged native for further examination, inserting his finger and thumb
between the valves. The irate mollusc, thinking, no
doubt, that this was meant as a further insult, snapped
its pearly doors down upon his fingers, causing him

considerable pain. After releasing his wounded digits, our inquisitive gentleman very naturally put them in his mouth. 'Delightful' exclaimed he, opening wide his eyes. 'What is this?' and again he sucked his fingers. Then the great truth flashed on him that he had found out a new delight – had, in fact, achieved the most important discovery ever made . . . and there and then, with no other condiment than its own juice, with no accompaniment of foaming brown stout or pale chablis to wash it down, no newly cut, well-buttered brown bread, did that solitary anonymous man inaugurate the first oyster banquet.[2]

George Frederick Watts, *Experientia Docet: Tasting the First Oyster*, 1882–3, oil on canvas.

Speculations about early human life reached a peak in the late nineteenth century, of course, with the impact of geological

'The First Oyster-
eater', from
*Chatterbox: Stories
of Natural History*,
1889.

discoveries, evolutionary theory and advancements in both
anthropology and archaeology, and all such speculations are
infused with gendered and racial assumptions. In 1882–3 the
artist G. F. Watts painted *Experientia Docet: Tasting the First
Oyster*, a large oil painting that portrays a prehistoric man and
woman sitting on a sea shore. The man has just opened and
swallowed an oyster; his face registers his disquiet; the woman
looks on quizzically. Watts, accused in reviews of being too
sombre, chose this subject apparently to show he could handle

lighter subjects, but it is difficult to see the humour here. Is it a failed meditation on the nature of desire or does Watts play on the oyster as a *fruit de mer*, a marine version of the apple that so tempted Eve? Here it is Adam and not Eve who tastes the first fruit.

Will knowledge come with the oyster as it did with the apple? An illustration in *Chatterbox: Stories of Natural History* of 1889, probably influenced by Watts's painting, provides another less grotesque version of prehistoric man's opening of the oyster. Here the woman has been removed and the man's disgust has been replaced with an expression of curious pleasure. His mouth is open, finger already in the oyster-shell. His heavy lids are almost closed in the pleasure of anticipation.

Such illustrations and meditations are complex, for the first oyster eater, conceived in these ways, forms a bridge between conceptions of the civilized and the barbaric, a bridge back into a primeval past. They seem to claim that just as the oyster has remained essentially the same in its functions and pleasures since deep time, so has man – at least in his love for oyster flesh. The smile on the face of the male oyster eater here, his curious touch of oyster flesh suspended in time, is also a marker of humanity's curiosity: as Figuier puts it, the oyster eater made 'the most important discovery'. These pictures express a degree of fascinated revulsion at the first oyster eater – *how could he?* – and at the same time an admiration: it is because of such curiosity that man has discovered so many of nature's secrets. When oyster eaters are animals, however, the story is quite different. Animal oyster eaters like the rat in La Fontaine's 'The Rat and the Oyster' are condemned as stupid and punished for their curiosity.

Oysters have also been the occasional subject of discourses on the nature of civilization, particularly in the seventeenth and eighteenth centuries when cannibalism stood as a marker of the opposition between the civilized and the barbaric.[3] Montaigne published an essay called 'On the Cannibals' in *The Essays, or Morall, Politicke, and Militarie Discourses* as early as 1580, and in *Robinson Crusoe*, for instance, published in 1719, the ship-wrecked Crusoe lives in fear of his life at the hands of cannibals and meditates upon the nature of barbarism.[4] He describes cannibalism as proof of 'the Horror of the Degeneracy of Humane Nature' and thanks God that he 'was distinguished from such dreadful Creatures'. In the mid-seventeenth century, the natural philosopher Robert Boyle scripted a dialogue in *Occasional Reflections* (1655) between two characters, Lindamor and Eugenius, on the practice of eating raw oysters, which he compares to the cannibalism of 'barbarians'. Lindamor maintains that:

> We impute it for a barbarous custom to many nations of the Indians that like beasts they eat raw flesh. And pray how much is that worse than our eating raw fish, as we do in eating these oysters? Nor is this a practice of the rude vulgar only, but of the politest and nicest persons amongst us, such as physicians, divines and even ladies. And our way of eating seems much more barbarous than theirs, since they are wont to kill before they eat, but we scruple not to devour oysters alive, and kill them not with our hands or teeth, but with our stomachs, where (for ought we know) they begin to be digested before they make an end of dying. Nay, sometimes when we dip them

in vinegar, we may, for sauce to one bit, devour alive a
shoal of little animals, which, whether they be fishes or
worms, I am not so sure, as I am, that I have by the help
of convenient glasses, seen great numbers of them swimming up and down in less than a saucer full of vinegar . . .
but I will demand, how much less we do ourselves, than
what we abominate in those savages, when we devour
oysters whole, guts, excrements and all? [5]

Lindamor argues that what marks out civilization from barbarism is the reluctance to eat living flesh. He seems not to be
making an argument for humankind to cook oysters or to kill
them more humanely but rather to be using the consumption of
raw oyster flesh by all members of society as a way of challenging absolute demarcations between the civilized and the barbaric and, by extension, some of the ideologies underpinning
the expansion of empire (how can we presume to be civilized?).
In this way Boyle's argument works in a similar way to the illustrations of the first oyster eater. For the oyster thus works as
a bridge between prehistoric man (supposedly barbaric) and
modern man (supposedly civilized) and a marker between 'us'
(civilized westerners) and 'them' (barbaric Indian tribes). It
isn't just the consumption of raw flesh that seems to be repellent but the consumption of raw, living flesh. It is disturbing; it
stimulates a degree of abjection; it strikes at what it means to be
human and distinct from the animals.

Other writers have used the consumption of raw, living
oyster flesh to prove the cruelty of man towards animals,
again as a means of challenging man's supposedly civilized
nature. In the late eighteenth century debates began to
emerge about the moral rights of animals in the wake of anti-
slavery campaigns and legislation. In 1781 Jeremy Bentham

published *An Introduction to the Principles of Morals and Legislation* in which he argued that animals should be given protection under the law, claiming that suffering was the vital characteristic that gives beings the right for legal consideration. The final sentence of his famous footnote has been much used since in animal rights campaigns: 'The question is not, Can they reason? Not can they talk? But can they suffer?'[6]

At around the same time, natural philosophers were trying to define the distinctions between the animal and vegetable worlds in relation to degrees of sensitivity to suffering. The characteristics of the animal were frequently defined as the ability to move at will, to feel / suffer and to digest. Yet there were animals and vegetables that seemed to defy these categories. The sea sponge, for instance, appeared to be completely inert and insensitive, whereas the mimosa, otherwise known as the sensitive plant, seemed to have sensitivity to touch. In the 1820s an Edinburgh physician, Robert Grant, conducted a series of experiments on the sea sponge to see if it reacted to pain: 'I have plunged portions of the branched and sessile sponges alive into acids, alcohol and ammonia, in order to excite their bodies to some kind of visible contractile motions, but have not produced by these powerful agents, any more effect upon the living specimens, than upon those which had long been dead'.[7]

In a poem by William Cowper (1731–1800), 'The Poet, The Oyster and the Sensitive Plant', the poet uses the oyster to philosophize on sensitivity and suffering in the animal and vegetable worlds. The poem opens with the oyster bemoaning its fate:

Ah hapless wretch! Condemned to dwell
For ever in my native shell,
Ordain'd to move when others please,

Not for my own content or ease,
But toss'd and buffeted about,
Now in the water, and now out.
'Twere better to be born a stone
Of ruder shape and feeling none,
Than with a tenderness like mine,
And sensibilities so fine!

The oyster's lamentation ends with a wish that its sensibilities might be as coarse as that of the mimosa it sees close by. The mimosa then scornfully replies that the oyster should make no such assumptions. She is a sensitive plant, much studied by botanists. Her excess of feeling, she claims, makes her more to be pitied than the oyster, for her life is 'spent, oh fie upon't! / In being touch'd, and crying, don't'. Now a poet in his evening walk joins the conversation arguing that: 'Your feelings in their full amount, / Are all upon your own account'.

You would not feel at all, not you.
The noblest minds that virtue prove
By pity, sympathy, and love,
These, these are feelings truly fine,
And prove their owner half divine.

His censure reach'd them as he dealt it,
And each by shrinking showed he felt it.[8]

In the same period in which natural philosophers were seeking to define the higher animals in relation to degrees of feeling, The Society for the Prevention of Cruelty to Animals was formed in London in 1824. Most of the Society's early legal battles and campaigns centred on domestic animals, particularly horses, dogs, cats and cattle. But the oyster had a small part to play in these disputes. After Parliament passed an 1822 bill preventing cruelty to animals, George Cruikshank caricatured a cookery writer, Dr Kitchiner, notorious for his greed for oysters, being arrested for eating oysters. But, more powerfully, in the early nineteenth century the French naturalist and animal campaigner M. Moquin-Tandon criticized the work of the SPCA for not being inclusive enough. Members were, he wrote, too concerned with domestic and territorial animals. Their arguments could be strengthened, he argued, by the widening of human compassion to include marine animals: if we are repelled by such suffering, how much worse is the suffering of the higher animals? To make his point, he anthropomorphized the oyster, telling its tale as a biography of suffering: in this tale the oyster is wrenched from his natural home, captured and taken to the cruel city to be sold. This is, of course, also a familiar narrative structure to those used in the anti-slavery campaigns. Here he describes the arrival of the enslaved oyster in London:

> This is a critical moment for the unhappy bivalve. Thrown into a tub of clean water, its hopes are cruelly revived, and for a moment it fancies its tortures are at an end, and once more it is in the sea. If ever it possessed such thoughts, they are soon dissipated, as it finds itself taken for the third and last time out of its native element. It is now in pitiless hands – a blunt knife, in spite of its most strenuous efforts, is thrust between its valves, and with a horrible wrench its shells are forced asunder. The muscle by which they were closed is cut or rather jagged through, and the hinges are violently detached. It is now laid on a plate, exposed to every current of the air, and in this state of suffering it is carried to the table. There the thoughtless

being for whose pleasure it has suffered untold woes, squeezes over its wounded and bleeding body the abomination of its race, the acrid vinegar; and then, alas! with a silver knife, which only jags but cannot cut, he wounds and bruises it a second time; or worse still, he saws and tears and rends it from its remaining shell; then he impales it with a three-pronged fork, and – horrible dictu! – still living and palpitating, he throws it into his mouth, where the teeth cut, and crush, and grind it'.[9]

OYSTER FLESH: COOKED, RAW AND ABJECT

Whilst there are those who have been morally repelled by oyster consumption, there are many more who have been physically repelled. There are three types of people in the world as far as oysters are concerned: those who love oysters, those who are indifferent to them and those who are passionately revolted by them. The nineteenth-century novelist William Makepeace Thackeray, for instance, found oysters abject. When, like Dickens, he visited New York, he was fêted as a celebrated author. Invited to the Centurion Club, he was given the usual Centurion dinner: saddlerock oysters, nearly as large as a dinner-plate. Thackeray is reputed to have paled and then whispered to his host 'What do I do with this animal?' to which his host replied 'We Americans swallow them whole'. Thackeray closed his eyes and swallowed the oyster. When his host enquired how he had liked the 'animal', Thackeray replied politely that it had been 'like swallowing a live baby'.[10] Later, in *Vanity Fair*, he described Mrs Frederick Bullock's kiss as like 'the contact of an oyster' (chapter 11).

So when Woody Allen most famously claimed 'I will not eat oysters. I want my food dead – not sick, not wounded – dead',

he was expressing a feeling of physical revulsion towards the oyster which has been shared by many since the first oyster eaters. When oysters are mentioned in conversation, faces light up or grimace. There is a 'how could you?' in the air for those who have never tasted raw oysters and will never do so, because the thought conjures dark thoughts – abject thoughts. In *Powers of Horror* the philosopher Julia Kristeva meditates on abjection as a 'violent, dark revolt of being, directed against a threat that seems to emanate from outside'. Food revulsions are the most elementary and the most archaic of abjections, she claims: 'It is not lack of cleanliness or health that causes abjection but what disturbs identity, system, order. What does not respect borders, positions, rules. The in-between, the ambiguous, the composite'.[11] Later she claims again that 'Food becomes abject only if it is a border between two distinct entities or territories. A boundary between nature and culture, between the human and the non-human'.[12]

Western culture is underpinned by a series of binaries between, for example, sun and moon, male and female, light and dark, cooked and raw, land and sea, civilized and barbaric, culture and nature; within each of these binaries is an implicit assumed superiority of the first of the pair over the second. The cultural anthropologist Claude Lévi-Strauss reminds us that because of such deep structures in language and myth, the raw is always associated with nature and the cooked with culture. The oyster, raw food of both epicure and savage, from the sea, looking at the same time both like an open wound and sexual organs, reminiscent of the translucence of flesh and bodily fluids, sits on that border between culture and nature and between male and female, between land and sea, between cooked and raw.

Oyster farmer eating oysters in the US in the 1960s.

But as Sigmund Freud and Mikhail Bakhtin remind us, the abject, the repressed or the repellent object in society (whether it is bodily fluids, sexual organs or revolting food) is also a source of rich comedy. The oyster is an interesting example of Bakhtin's grotesque body in that it echoes and shadows sexual organs, wounds and raw – even bruised – flesh. The comic American writer and journalist Roy Blount Jr wrote a poem in the 1940s in which the comedy turns precisely on the tension between desire and revulsion which the oyster frequently provokes:

SONG TO OYSTERS

I like to eat an uncooked oyster.
Nothing's slicker, nothing's moister.
Nothing's easier on your gorge
Or when the time comes, to disgorge.
But not to let it too long rest
Within your mouth is always best.
For if your mind dwells on an oyster . . .
Nothing's slicker. Nothing's moister.
I prefer my oyster fried.
Then I'm sure my oyster's died.

But Anne Stevenson's poem, 'Oysters', published in 2000, turns, in a much more sinister, and to my mind more successful, way on the conjunction between flesh, sex and death that the oyster stimulates in the most social and intimate of places: the restaurant. In this poem, fattened oyster flesh slips easily into fattened human flesh; laughter echoes, but so does death, enshrined in the references to the crypt of the basilisk dress that encases the dangerously alluring flesh of the man's fleshy companion. In an extraordinary slippage, the woman's breasts, bearing a diamond brooch, become dunes on a beach where oysters grow fat on sewage – so that we are reminded that this oyster being consumed has grown fat and radioactive on human waste. This is all quite 'beyond the laughable' as poisoned flesh slips into poisoned flesh in an endless cycle of poisoned and poisoning nature:

the fat man laughed because
the restaurant told him to,
though the oysters that slipped
at atrocious expense
through his pinguid lips
were poisonous,
and the hock at his elbow
hardly less,
and the lady too,
so svelte in the crypt
of her basilisk dress
was dangerous
beyond the laughable.
Wasn't that diamond
clipped at her cleavage
an oyster between
white dunes on a beach,
grown luscious on sewages
steamy tureen
of barely detectable
radioactive garbage?[13]

6 Oyster Philosophies

Oyster-shells tell of time; they are the silent witnesses of an early world that rang with the sound of the hunting cries of scaly lizards long before the evolution of mammals that would become recognizably human. And later, when humans built their first encampments on rocky shorelines and in sheltered inlets, they left behind piles of discarded oyster-shells – the remains of their smoky oyster feasts – to mark their passing. Geologists use fossilized oyster-shells to date rock strata; archaeologists use oyster middens to date early human settlements. Charles Darwin searched for fossil oyster-beds in South America, for he knew that when continents cracked and severed and drifted apart millions of years ago, oyster-beds had moved with them.

When Victorian naturalists began to accept and develop the idea of the evolution of species, they used fossil evidence – the fragments of bones and plants and animal fossils and rock samples piled in museums – to try to imagine what they called 'deep time', a world before human habitation, populated by monsters. Oysters and other shellfish appear in many of these nineteenth-century paintings and drawings, as Martin Rudwick has shown in *Scenes of Deep Time*. For the Victorian observer, the existence of oysters in these pictures of deep time must have created a kind of temporal dislocation, for they would have been looking at a bafflingly strange landscape populated by fierce and alien creatures such as the pterodactyl and tyrannosaur and yet at the same time full of that most familiar of nineteenth-century urban street objects, the oyster.

In the light of geological evidence and evolutionary ideas, then, the oyster began to be understood differently in the nineteenth century, as a creature which had predated man's arrival on the planet by possibly millions of years. Natural philosophers began to use the oyster as the object of meditations on the nature of time or survival. In these philosophical narratives oysters were heroic; they had out-survived the great lumbering carnivorous species, had found a way of adapting to their environment so that few further changes had been necessary in millions of years. The American lawyer and judge James Watson Gerard, for instance, published this stanza in a longer poem about the oyster in his satirical work *Ostrea; or the Loves of Oysters,* published in New York in 1857:

I sing the Oyster! (Virgin Theme!)
King of Molluscules! Ancient of the stream!
Thy birth was Time's – soon as th' affrighted world,
A quivering mass, in space immense was hurled –
In darkness cradled – mid chaos nursed
Tumultuous! – Ambiguous, till burst
Thy unctuous beauty on a world where none
Could know they merit; there, alone
Thou pineds't forlorn, 'mid mud and flood and slime
Ere man came on the stage, far in the time
Cosmogenetical.[1]

At the same time increasingly powerful microscopes showed how complex and beautifully adapted the oyster's small body

This rusty bicycle, covered in oysters, was retrieved from the sea at the French town of Marennes in May 1990.

was. Now evolutionary naturalists, seeing it much magnified, wondered at the sophistication of its evolutionary strategies in public lectures, using the oyster as a way of popularizing evolutionary ideas. Thomas Huxley, charismatic and imaginative popularizer of Darwin's ideas, for instance, described it in the 1880s: 'I suppose that when the sapid and slippery morsel – which is gone like a flash of gustatory summer lightning – glides along the palate, few people imagine that they are swallowing a piece of machinery (and going machinery too) greatly more complicated than a watch'.[2] Huxley could assume that his audience – rich and poor – would be familiar with the anatomy of the oyster – most would have eaten oysters regularly, would have remembered levering open the shell of an oyster with a knife, and some might have already contemplated the oyster's anatomy at close hand before they tipped up the shell and slithered its flesh into their mouths.

Other nineteenth-century naturalists, writing in a tradition of natural theology, worked hard to maintain the hierarchies of

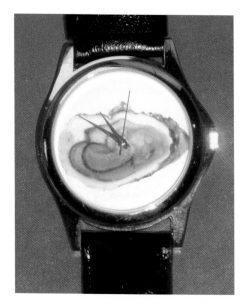

A novelty oyster watch, made in China in 2004. Rolex launched the classic 'oyster' range of watches in 1926 – the first wristwatches to be considered water-proof.

nature now threatened by evolutionary ideas. They were determined to see God's work in the oyster and to argue for a nature characterized by *fixed* hierarchies. From the observation of such lower creatures, natural theologians could sermonize on 'right' ways of living within nature, arguing for instance that if you look at nature you can see that God has made each organism to 'know its place' within a hierarchy with man at its pinnacle. An anonymous poet from the Preston 'Oyster and Parched Pea Club' satirized this tradition of using nature to tell the working man to stay in his place in a poem on the oyster published in 1816 in the *Preston Chronicle*:

A something monastic appears amongst oysters,
For gregarious they live, yet they sleep in their cloisters;
'Tis observed too, that oysters, when placed in their barrel,

Will never presume with their stations to quarrel.
From this let us learn what an oyster can tell us,
And we all shall be better and happier fellows.
Acquiesce in your stations, whenever you've got 'em;
Be not proud at the top, nor repine at the bottom,
Be happier they in the middle who live,
And have something to lend, and to spend and to give.[3]

By the middle of the nineteenth century oysters were being used, then, to argue for or illustrate different versions of nature – one God-ordained and fixed, the other in a process of constant mutability. They were used to muse on time, or on harmonious adaptation to environment, or on progress, or to moralize on divinely ordained ways of living. This knowledge helps to make sense of certain peculiarities in Victorian culture, such as the fact that when Mary Ann Evans (later George Eliot) and John Chapman relaunched the *Westminster Review* in 1852 as a

Mr Beville of Great Wakering, Essex, shows off his unusual model of Canterbury Cathedral constructed from oyster shells. The model contains 660 shells and took four months to build in the 1930s.

radical journal dedicated to publishing philosophical and political ideas about progress, they commissioned for the first edition an article from the Scottish naturalist and mollusc expert Edward Forbes on – of all things – shellfish. 'Shell-fish: Their Ways and Works' was published alongside articles on employment rights and representative reform.

Forbes' shellfish article is one of the most lyrical pieces of mid-nineteenth-century natural history writing. Most of it is a kind of prose poem about oysters. Forbes could assume both that his readers had seen oysters close up and also that they had overlooked their extraordinary anatomy and ancestry. He begins:

Look at an oyster. In what light does the world in general – not your uneducated, stolid world merely, but your refined, intellectual, cultivated, classical world – regard it? Simply as a delicacy – as good to eat. The most devoted of oyster-eaters opens the creature's shell solely to swallow the included delicious morsel, without contemplation or consideration . . . And yet there is a philosophy in oyster-shells undreamed of by the mere conchologist! A noble and wondrous philosophy revealing to us glimpses of the creative power among the dim and distant abysses of the incalculable past, speaking to us of the genesis of oyster-creatures ere the idea of man occupied the creative mind; giving us a scale by which to measure the building up of the world in which we live, such as the mathematician and the natural philosopher, and the astronomer, all combining, could not furnish; unfolding for us the pages of the volume in which the history of our planet, its convulsions and tranquilities, its revolutions and gradualities, are inscribed in unmistakable characters.

For Forbes the lesson of successful adaptation illustrated by the oyster is not 'stay in your place' but 'enjoy life' for, he argues, the oyster shows us that an organism in happy harmony with its surroundings is one that will survive:

> In that soft and gelatinous body lies a whole world of vitality and quiet enjoyment. An undisturbed oyster-bed is a concentration of happiness in the present . . . each individual is leading the beatified existence of an Epicurean god. The world without – its cares and joys, its storms and calms, its passions, evil and good – all are indifferent to the unheeding oyster. Unobservant even of what passes in its immediate vicinity, its whole soul is concentrated in itself, yet not sluggishly and apathetically, for its whole body is throbbing with life and enjoyment.[4]

The oyster had become in Forbes's hands a model of an organism in successful and harmonious balance with its surroundings – a creature that knew its place but which was also adapting into a future. Interestingly, other writers around the same time portray oyster dredgers in a similar way, as if they are a natural extension of the oyster's harmony with its environment. In 1859, for instance, a curiously nostalgic article about oyster shops and oyster farmers appeared in Dickens's journal *All the Year Round*, entitled 'The Happy Fishing-ground'. Searching for a lost pre-industrial Englishness, the author finds it among the oyster dredgers of Whitstable. He refers to these people as

> incorporated free-fishers . . . joined together by the ties of a common birthplace, by blood, by marriage, capital

Curios from the collection of the late Johnny Noble, founder of Loch Fyne Oysters: an oyster plate in majolica, a Japanese oyster plate adorned with crabs, and one of a pair of four-tier revolving oyster-serving dishes, also in majolica.

and trade. It has always been their pride, from time out of mind, to live in these dwarfed huts on this stony beach, watching the happy fishing grounds that lie under the brackish water in the bay, where millions of oysters are always breeding with marvellous fertility, and all for incorporated company's good . . . They are all equal; they are all working together for good. The father meets his son . . . the nephew meets his uncle, the uncle meets his cousin, the cousin inquires after his aunt, who is laid up with lumbago; the grandson lends a helping hand to his grandfather; the brother-in-law is in attendance upon his relations by marriage, and the whole scene is a picture of quiet, profitable, patriarchal trade . . . They have lived amongst oysters, and thought of them so long, till, at last, it is possible to trace something of that steady, stationary shell-fish in their nature. They have fallen upon favourable ground where they fatten and thrive; they show no disposition to wander and move.[5]

The writer's romantic portrayal of the oyster dredgers as a relic of old England, the embodiment of lost values, is typical of this period of rapid industrialization and of social unrest in the lead-up to the Second Reform Act which would enfranchise the working man in 1867. This romantic piece is full of class anxiety in its celebration of the oyster-dredging community and this is hardly surprising at a time when a large number of the middle and ruling classes were concerned about the future of a country in which supposedly uneducated workers would be given the vote. But it also strives to reassure – these simple people are the backbone of an older England. They are good citizens; they know their place; they are not to be feared.

The notion, however, that man might have evolved from primitive sea creatures, as some comparative anatomists had been proposing since the end of the eighteenth century, filled many nineteenth-century intellectuals with revulsion. Several writers used the notion of man's evolution from the oyster as a way of pouring scorn on evolutionary ideas. In *Silver-Shell; or, the Adventures of an Oyster* (1856), for instance, the Revd Williams writes with ridicule: 'And so it has been said, by a series of transitions the monad became an oyster, the oyster a monkey, and the monkey a man.'[6] And in the months that followed the publication of Charles Darwin's *On the Origin of Species by means of Natural Selection* in 1859, the oyster was again used to mock Darwin's ideas. In January 1860, for instance, Jane Carlyle wrote to a friend:

But even when Darwin, in a book that all the scientific world is in ecstasy over, proved the other day that we are all come from shell-fish, it didn't move me to the slightest curiosity whether we are or not. I did not feel that the slightest light would be thrown on my practical life for me, by having it ever so logically made out that my first ancestor, millions of millions of years back, had been, or even had not been, an oyster. It remained a plain fact that I was no oyster, nor had any grandfather an oyster within my knowledge; and for the rest, there was nothing to be gained, for this world or the next, by going into the oyster-question, till all more pressing questions were exhausted.[7]

In the following year – 1861 – the marine painter Edward William Cooke, who had a special interest in geology and the new biological sciences, went to a meeting of the British

AD ARMA PARATUS.   QUOD RETIS HIC EST.   CURRENTE CALAMO

Edward William Cooke, 'Darwin Animals', a plate from his *Grotesque Animals Invented, Drawn and Described* (London, 1872). The head of the middle figure is an oyster shell.

Association for the Advancement of Science (BAAS) in Manchester. The discussions that year in the wake of the publication of Darwin's *On the Origin of Species by means of Natural Selection* were all about human–animal kinship. Cooke described in his journal how he was suddenly overcome by a sense of revulsion and misanthropy standing amongst all the well-dressed men and women discussing Darwin's book, as he imagined their kinship to animals. He fled the meeting and took himself off to the seaside where over the next few weeks, suffering a degree of fascinating existentialist disgust, he drew a series of animal–human caricatures that he called his 'Darwin creatures' and which he published as a Christmas book in 1872 called *Grotesque Animals Invented, Drawn and Described*.

Cooke's grotesques were, of course, drawn in the tradition of Jean-Ignace Gérard Grandville and Paul Gavarni, but they have a peculiarly late nineteenth-century nightmare vision about them. The animals are drawn to look like humans standing talking to each other, much as Cooke would have seen them at the BAAS meeting, but they are made up of human / animal body parts, most of which are drawn from sea creatures, including oysters, rather than apes as one might have expected.

By the late nineteenth century the idea of human–animal kinship began to take on a darker quality of nightmare in the hands of the science-fiction writer H. G. Wells, who had been trained as a zoologist. Wells's fictional monsters are often slimy and tentacled. When someone is asked to describe the Martian invaders in *War of the Worlds*, for instance, the closest they can come to an analogy is an octopus. Giant crabs stalk the time-traveller; the Morlocks are a strange hybrid of ape and marine creature; Dr Moreau works on making animal–human hybrids through vivisection; and the final vision the time-traveller sees at the end of time itself is a tentacled creature hopping about fitfully in the waves of a blood-red sea.

The possibility of degeneration took a while to dawn: if some species had evolved, others become extinct, might not others be moving backwards? And just as oysters had been used to embody evolutionary progress at mid-century, now they could be used by late nineteenth-century writers to exemplify degeneracy. In 1880, for instance, the marine zoologist and moral prophet Edwin Ray Lankester claimed in *Degeneration: A Chapter in Darwinism* that until recently naturalists had assumed that all organisms either *improve* or *stay the same*. But, he argued, there was also a third way – degeneration – and he listed oysters, sponges, polyps, starfishes, coral animals, mussels and clams as examples of degenerated creatures. He was determined to make sure his readers understood the moral lesson:

Any new set of conditions occurring to an animal which render its food and its safety very easily attained, seem to lead as a rule to Degeneration; just as an active healthy man sometimes degenerates when he becomes suddenly possessed of a fortune; or as Rome degenerated when possessed of the riches of the ancient world. The habit of parasitism clearly acts upon animal organisation in this way. Let the parasitic life once be secured, and away go legs, jaws, eyes and ears; the active, highly gifted crab, insect, or annelid may become a mere sac, absorbing nourishment and laying eggs.[8]

And the object of this moral lesson for Lankester was the aristocracy. He believed that, leisured and lacking the need to compete for food, the aristocracy were now parasitic and degenerating. Like the Romans, life for the oysters and for British aristocracy had became too easy, the food supply too rich. In Lankester's hands, oysters had become an object lesson in the work ethic, a warning against parasitism.

Nineteenth-century natural philosophers were all in their different ways committed to asking 'what is natural?', 'what is progress?' and 'how can we learn from nature's apparent laws?' How apt then that at the heart of all their empirical practices and abstract speculations should be found embedded that most nineteenth-century of creatures – the oyster. But of course nature's laws are as difficult to read as the oyster itself, which means that – depending on what was being argued – the oyster was used by nineteenth-century writers as an object lesson for a plethora of different and sometimes contradictory 'truths'.

In 1865 the French painter Edouard Manet, inspired by see-ing Velázquez's extraordinary paintings of Aesop and of other beggar-philosophers in the Prado in Madrid, painted his own

Edouard Manet,
*Philosopher
(Beggar with
Oysters)*, 1865–7,
oil on canvas.
Manet's painting
enigmatically
couples the
philosopher with
the oyster as
apparently
commonplace
but invisibly
complex.

pair of philosophers. In the second of the two, entitled simply *Philosopher* (Art Institute of Chicago), Manet painted an old man who stands looking out at us against a black background. Only two pools of light emerge from this magnificent range of blacks, greys and browns: the upper part of the philosopher's face and eyes and the gleaming white flesh of two opened oysters, which stand out against the brown pile of oyster-shells in the bottom right-hand corner. The oysters, of course, suggest the philosopher's lowly status and his simple street food, but it also marks out his strangeness. Beggars, Manet reminds us, though they are, like oyster-shells, ubiquitous and overlooked, can be philosophers. Appearances are often deceptive; the rough brown shell may bear no relation to the astonishingly delicate and complex interior. Once again Manet has used the oyster to embody the drama of the *seemingly* commonplace, and indeed to challenge the very notion of the commonplace itself.

7 Oyster Arts

Why did certain Dutch and Flemish artists in the seventeenth century stop painting madonnas and saints and begin instead to paint the commonplace objects around them: men and women eating or sitting in conversation in cool, shadowed interiors where the light catches the rim of a spinning wheel or wineglass, the sheen of a grape or the gleam of a pearl? And why did others abandon the human form entirely to compose richly shadowed and textured still lifes of bread, oysters, wine, fruit and meat, now the enthroned subjects of their own space and time?

For a short time in the seventeenth century, in the Low Countries, the oyster, until now neglected in Western art, found its place in oil paintings alongside lemons, fruit, silver platters or glasses of champagne, each object distilled against a crow-black background. In these *still-leven*, or still-lifes, the complex whites of oyster flesh gleam and shimmer, next to the nacreous whites of mother-of-pearl, against the russet-blue-whites of oyster-shells. Why was the oyster summoned into paint for the short-lived decades of the *still-leven*'s ascendancy? What part did the oyster have to play? What did these pictures mean?

The art historian Liana de Girolami Cheney proposes that the oyster is used as a symbol in Dutch and Flemish seven-teenth-century art and – as symbol – the oyster's meanings change through the century.[1] Oysters first appeared, she says,

Frans Floris de Vriendt, *Feast of the Gods*, 1550, oil on panel.

when Flemish painters painting the popular 'feast of the gods' in the sixteenth century represented it as a bacchanal in which the gods banquet voluptuously amongst discarded oyster-shells. In 1550, for instance, Frans Floris painted his *Feast of the Gods* with Jupiter reaching for an oyster, Aphrodite sitting on a large oyster-shell and Cupid cupping an oyster in his hand, his arrows fallen to the ground. The oysters mark the gods' pleasure but also their excess and abandon. The painter, by showing us these gods naked, exposed and opened up, seems to want to show us how vulnerable even divine flesh becomes in the experience of pleasure.

When early seventeenth-century painters transformed the feast of the gods genre into contemporary 'merry company' scenes, replacing naked gods with well-dressed Dutch men and women in domesticated interiors, they retained the implied moral warnings about the consequences of pleasure. In Dirck Hals's *A Party at Table* of 1625, for instance, a painting hanging on the wall behind the men and women feasting on oysters depicts the *Expulsion from Paradise*. The opulence of the company is emphasized by their dress and again by the discarded oyster-shells on the floor. Pleasure is transitory, the picture intones.

After 1660 in the Low Countries, paintings of people eating oysters grow more intimate. Now fewer men and women eat oysters in smaller domestic interiors, the parlour or the bedroom rather than in the dining room. Now there are at most three people eating, usually only two – a man and a woman. The light falls on the couple eating; they are framed more tightly within the composition. The 'camera' draws closer, lingering.

In Frans van Mieris's *Oyster Dinner* (overleaf), for instance, the scene is significantly and intensely erotic: the woman's jacket falls open to reveal flesh, and the oyster satin in which she is dressed falls loosely over her opened legs with a sheen like the mother-of-pearl of the oysters themselves,. She cups the oyster exquisitely in her hand, wine glass in the other, as the older man leans forward to whisper words to her. Behind them the bed curtains wait to be opened. What did the painted oyster offered in the bedroom say to its seventeenth-century viewers? It is difficult to say: that once opened perhaps, innocence is not to be closed again, or that pleasures are transitory?

In Jan Steen's *Young Girl Eating Oysters* of 1658–60 (overleaf), the 'camera' draws closer yet. The woman oyster eater, sprinkling salt or pepper on her food, looks up at us alluringly, as if she knows the viewer desires her, and as if she has been caught in an illicit act for which she feels no shame. The oyster

Frans van Mieris, *Oyster Dinner*, 1661, oil on wood.

and its eater seem to be composed here for admiration's sake, intimate, seductive – they appear to carry no moral censure. Yet in his *Easy Come, Easy Go*, (1661, Museum Boymans-van Beuningen, Rotterdam) Steen used discarded oyster-shells alongside several other emblems in the painting to point a very explicit moral: in the back room two men are playing back-gammon, the dog sniffs the lemon that will taste sour to his

Jan Steen, *Young Girl Eating Oysters*, c. 1658–60, oil on panel.

tongue, one painting depicts a shipwreck, another a statue of fortune standing on a die resting on a winged globe. Difficult not to follow this Protestant message: money, virtue, success are all easily acquired and easily lost. Spend wisely.

And then there are seventeenth-century paintings in which the 'camera' draws even closer, erasing all human presence, and these are even more difficult for the twenty-first century viewer

135

to decode. 'Breakfast-pieces', or still-lifes of food, are unique to seventeenth-century north-west European art and were almost all produced by artists working in Antwerp, Frankfurt, Haarlem and Amsterdam between 1630 and 1700. Here the food objects are disconnected from human life. They seem to have found silence, to have shaken off their moral significance and to exist just for themselves, oysters for oysters' sake, or at least for the sake of white flesh tones cupped in mother-of-pearl and in roughened, petticoated white; desirable.

Osias Beert (1570–1624), a Flemish painter who worked in Antwerp, was one of the greatest oyster still-life painters of the early seventeenth century, but we know frustratingly little about him or about why he began to paint breakfast-pieces. Only eight of his paintings have survived; several place the dish of oysters at centre stage. In his *Bodegón* ('tavern scene') in the Prado, Madrid, for instance, a fly sits on the loaf of fresh bread

Osias Beert the Elder, *Bodegón* (*Oysters and Glasses*), c. 1610. oil on panel.

– its presence reminds us that the process of decomposition is held, but even now in this timelessness the fly has already begun to feed and lay its eggs, the opening oysters are already turning. Time passes, flesh decays. But paradoxically the oyster painter has stopped time, sealed it in paint, just as he asks us to contemplate time's passing. In another Beert oyster piece, in the Staatsgalerie in Stuttgart, a flake of a pastry has fallen onto the foreground of the table, looking for all the world like a maggot. The oysters held in time, 'still to be enjoy'd', evoke lines from Keats's 'Ode on a Grecian Urn', in which the poet contemplates an urn on which painted lovers pursue each other. Keats shows us how the lovers are immortalized in the act of love, but also held back by art from its consummation:

Osias Beert the Elder, *Banquet Piece with Oysters, Fruit and Wine*, c. 1610/20, oil on panel.

For ever warm and still to be enjoy'd,
For ever panting, and for ever young;
All breathing human passion far above,
That leaves a heart high-sorrowful and cloy'd,
A burning forehead, and a parching tongue.

Osias Beert was also an innovator in terms of form. Other early 'breakfast-piece' painters tended to take a higher viewpoint, grouping their objects simply in tiered rows. Instead Beert saw an opportunity for compositional experiments: glasses upright and upturned echo each other, the oval shapes of the oysters echo lemon ovals and those of nuts and olives.

Later in the seventeenth century, the Haarlem artists Pieter Claesz. (c. 1597–1661) and Willem Claesz. Heda (1594–1680) began to experiment with the genre, by lowering the viewpoint so that the eye rests on a level with the object, emphasizing outline against a stark background, as Beert had done. But unlike Beert, Claesz. and Heda toned down colour to experiment with monochromes (shades of grey, silver, brown-lilac, grey-whites), playing with different illuminative effects from clear daylight to artificial light and *chiaroscuro*. They moved their oysters around on the table in order to experiment with balance, weighting the objects in the space towards one side or the other and reducing the number of food objects so that we look more closely. Here, as in Beert's work, time has been sealed – the table is in disarray, someone has begun to eat the food, but for a moment we have been asked to look and admire the beauty of the disarray.

These oyster paintings are enigmatic. They appear to be full of codes and yet are so difficult to read. And, of course, even the breakfast-pieces are not really *still*-lifes – nothing here is still. Action presses forward. Everything is moving, turning. But why

are we asked to look at oysters – or for that matter, loaves, fishes, olives? In *The Art of Describing: Dutch Art in the Seventeenth Century* (1983), Svetlana Alpers argues that the common practice of Dutch still-life painting is

Willem Claesz. Heda, *Still-life with Oysters, Rum Glass and Silver Cup*, 1634, oil on panel.

> to reveal to our sight . . . Whether it is edibles such as cheese, a pie, herring, fruit or nuts, or collectibles such as shells, vessels, and watches, we are offered the inside, or underside as well as the outer view. Cheeses are cut into, pies spill out their fillings beneath the shelter of crust, herring are cut to reveal flesh as well as gleaming skins. Shells and vessels of precious metal or glasses topple on their sides . . . and watches are inevitably opened to

reveal their works. Objects are exposed to the probing eye not only by the technique of flaying them, but also by reflection: the play of light on the surface distinguishes glass from metal, from cloth, from pastry, and also serves to multiply surfaces.[2]

These objects, she argues, demand that we look and discriminate between the identities of things. She links this invitation to look closely to the influence of Sir Francis Bacon's *Advancement of Learning*, published in 1605. Bacon argues:

> Those, however, who aspire not to guess and divine, but to discover and know; who propose not to devise mimic and fabulous worlds of their own, but to examine and dissect the nature of the world itself; must go to facts for everything.[3]

But the breakfast-pieces did not enjoin the viewer to look closely at *everything*. The objects collected in a *still-life* were particular because they were ordinary – familiar, everyday, and, in the words of the art historian Norman Bryson, therefore *overlooked*. In *Looking at the Overlooked: Four Essays on Still Life Painting* (1990) he writes:

> Still life takes in the exploration of what "importance' tramples underfoot . . . The human figure, with all of its fascination, is expelled. Narrative – the drama of greatness – is banished. And what is looked at overturns the standpoint on which human importance is established. Still life is unimpressed by the categories of achievement, grandeur and the unique.[4]

There is drama here even in the most ordinary of objects, these painters seem to insist – in the play of light, in the range of tones and colours and in the structural and geometric relationships between the arranged objects.

Jean-Baptiste-Siméon Chardin, *The Ray*, 1728, oil on canvas.

In 1728 the young French painter Jean-Baptiste-Siméon Chardin (1699–1779) painted an extraordinary composition called *The Ray*. Indebted to Dutch art in its attention to the overlooked, it nonetheless shows, on closer examination, an entirely different set of brushstrokes, loose, rugged and aggressive. It is a violent picture but also a kitchen scene, which like the work of the Dutch *still-leven* painters reminds us that nothing is ordinary and nothing stands still. This too tells us to look

– to turn our gaze into a quiet familiar corner where something remarkable – and terrible – is happening. A cat, teeth bared, stalks oysters on a kitchen shelf; behind her a ray hangs suspended against stone by a hook, its flesh ruddy and bleeding, its 'face' grotesque and grimacing; a knife jags inwards into the picture space; a few inches away a dead fish juts towards us, it has died gasping for air. But in the midst of all this predatory violence, a heap of white linen invites our eyes to linger on the beauty of its folds.

What Chardin and the earlier still-life painters in the Low Countries have in common is that they show us the drama of the commonplace, remind us to look in corners we had not perhaps noticed before, and then to look again. George Eliot would learn this in the mid-nineteenth century in her travels to

opposite:
Jan Davidsz. de Heem, *Still Life with a Glass and Oysters, c.* 1640, oil on wood.

Hannah Collins, *Sex, No. 1,* 1991, gelatin-silver print mounted on cotton.

Bianca Sforni, *Oyster Portrait XI*, from a series of twelve oyster portraits taken in 1993.

northern Europe and in her contemplation of Dutch art. These quiet paintings also reminded her about something she already knew – the stories she wanted to tell were not of the extraordinary lives of great men and women, but of the commonplace men and women she had observed around her. These lives were to be looked at; they were like still-lifes, but never still. This was the drama of the overlooked.

In *Still Life with Oysters and Lemon*, the poet Mark Doty describes memory as working like a still-life painting: 'a poetic field of objects arrayed against the dark, things somehow conjoined in a conspiracy of silence, some whispered communion between them, a dialogue we cannot hear'.[5] Like Bolitho he tells of falling in love with oysters – painted oysters – in a still-life by the eighteenth-century Dutch painter Davidsz. de Heem, called *Still-life with a Glass and Oysters*. And he describes the desire that Osias Beert's painted oyster flesh draws from him, a desire to turn them into words and to have these words – like the oysters themselves – *on his tongue*:

> When it came to oysters, Osias Bert had no peer, I think. In the National Gallery of Art in Washington there is a platter of his oysters that seems the ultimate expression of light playing on the slightly viscous, pearly, opalescent, and convoluted flesh, its wetness distinguishing it from the similarly sheened but hard stuff of the shell's interior. Their liquidity makes me want language to match, want on my tongue their deliquescence, their liquefaction.[6]

The peeled lemons and the oysters in de Heem's painting are intimate, as if undressed, he writes: 'they are, in a way, nudes, always in dishabille, partly undraped, the rind peeled away to allow our gaze further pleasure – to see the surface, and beneath that another surface'.[7] But, he concludes, what ultimately distinguishes still-life paintings is a tension between the super-real materiality of the objects and their dissolution, their aloofness and silence: 'they satisfy so deeply because they offer us intimacy and distance at once, allow us to be both here and gone'.[8] He quotes Jules David Prown writing about Raphaelle Peale's *Fruit in a Basket*: 'Of what do still-lives speak? Of relationships – connections, reflections, support, power, balance; of taste, touch and smell; of man and nature, of markets and appetites and genetics and diet; of time, mortality, and regeneration. If we are to understand what a still-life signifies, we must attend closely.'

What might Claesz and Heda have done with oysters had they had access to modern cameras, zoom lenses and electric light? The British Turner Prize nominee Hannah Collins and the Milanese artist Bianca Sforni are contemporary photographers who have been drawn into the oyster spell. Just as Claesz. and Heda turned to more and more monochrome effects in order to pursue the whites and greys of oyster flesh and the gleam of mother-of-pearl, so these painters also work in black and white. By bringing in the frame more tightly on oyster flesh, they ask us to attend even more closely. If seventeenth-century painters had used the oyster to signify sex, desire, hunger and flesh within an elaborate emblem system, oysters, for these twentieth-century women photographers, become the embodiment of the naked flesh of sex itself. Hannah Collins' *Sex, No. 1* (1991), though very specifically titled, is cool and restrained. Oyster water drips out of each of these shallow pools. By placing closed and open oysters together, Collins makes us look at surfaces and depths, inside and outside, hard and soft, all transformed into a spectrum of tones of white through to black, only the dark shadows of seeping fluid breaking the picture frame. Bianca Sforni's

oyster 'portraits', grainy matte-textured photographs two feet high, have been described as 'sexualised enough to make Mapplethorpe's lilies blush'. Oyster flesh, wet and gaping, fills the frame like an opened flower. An enthusiastic reviewer of her 1993 show at the Paul Kasmin Gallery in New York wrote: 'In this swooningly, almost comically erotic fantasy, the famously aphrodisiac animals are shown pried wide open, the freshly exposed flesh all labial fold and pucker . . . they are so vividly wet they seem to positively warp the paper . . . the oysters come as close to pornography as metaphorical imagery can'.[9]

For other artists, fleshless oyster-shells have been a way of exploring timeless structures for whilst oyster flesh speaks of sex

Paul Hill, *Hard to Swallow*, 2002, metal.

Philip Ross,
Oyster sculpture,
Tomales Bay,
California, 2002–3
(after cleaning).

and mutability, oyster-shells speak of eternity. Paul Hill, for instance, an American sculptor from North Carolina, makes actual-size oyster-shells from burnished metal, exploring shapes, folds and colours.[10] The metal, highly polished, catches the light as mother-of-pearl does, so the matt, craggy textures of natural oyster-shells are turned inside out by polished complex layerings. Suddenly oysters become metallic crinolines.

Between the summers of 2000 and 2002 the sculptor Philip Ross, a Stanford University lecturer and an artist-in-residence at San Francisco's Exploratorium science museum, began work on a large oyster sculpture at the Johnson oyster-farm in Tomales Bay, California. He constructed a 23-foot-long metal frame in the shape of the upturned hull of a ship or the ribcage of a huge animal and immersed it in the oyster-spat-rich waters of the Johnson oyster-farm. Young oysters – Ross calls them him 'little minions' – made their home here on the smooth metal, which was designed to oxidize and disappear in the water over two years.[11] The matured oysters, as their metal bed disappeared from under them, were of course all joined to each other in the shape of the upturned ship's hull. After three years Ross returned to haul up his oyster wreck from the seabed. A friend described the scene:

the oysters were barely identifiable as themselves as they were covered in a thick oozing seaweed. Of course, it wasn't green seaweed but a colour more reminiscent of something internal, bodily – perhaps not unlike how I imagine the pancreas, the lining of the stomach, the

Philip Ross,
Oyster sculpture,
Tomales Bay
(before cleaning)

mucus from a 100-foot giant, the slime from the hugest of oozing scabs – all pink and orange and fleshy and drippy. Really disgusting. Once they were placed on the barge a zillion crabs and eels started leaping to the floor, flopping around and scuttling to find a crevice in which to hide. It went on like this.

The final piece, cleaned and bleached white, now stands in the museum – a man-made fossil and upturned wreck, still and quiet, quite different from the grotesque slithering eco-system that emerged from the seabed.

In 2001 the installation artist Stephen Turner devised a series of oyster grottoes in Whitstable and along London's Tower Bridge foreshore in the tradition of the oyster grottoes built by Victorian

Stephen Turner's *Grotta* on the foreshore at Whitstable in Kent, 2001.

children at the beginning of the oyster season, lit by single candles. These wonderful oyster cairns, lit up on the waterside, hauntingly evoke shell middens and early human settlements.

The cock's comb oyster (*Lopha cristagalli*).

Oyster-shells have also provided the inspiration for several iconic architectural designs of the twentieth century. The craggy, jagged, zigzagged shapes of the giant cock's comb oyster (*Lopha cristagalli*) provided part of the natural inspiration for the Danish architect Jorn Utzon's design of the Sydney Opera House. The result of an international design contest won by Utzon in 1956, the massive structure perched on Bennelong Point took nearly 17 years and $102 million to complete. This extraordinary white-bleached building made of precast and tile-covered concrete juts out into the sea and is reflected in it on a headland where aborigines collected oysters long before

Sunrise over the Sydney Opera House. Jorn Utzon's design for the building, begun in 1957, was in part modelled on the craggy zigzags of the cock's comb oyster.

European settlers found their way here. It stands as a bridge, therefore, between the ancient and the modern, evoking the sea above in its visual echo of wind-blown fishing sails, and the sea below in its jutting oyster shapes.

Oysters are silent and enigmatic, but in the hands of painters, photographers, architects and installation artists they have come to speak of time, memory and desire. And when they have not been used as object lessons on the consequences of pleasure or to meditate on decay or the mysteries of time, they have been painted entirely for the sheens and textures of oyster-shells and oyster flesh – the challenge of capturing the effects of light on wet flesh and the lure of representing a whiteness that is never quite – or merely – white. The oyster, though ubiquitous and familiar, is – for the artist and writer trying to turn it into words or paint – never quite knowable, always just beyond representation.

'La Perle', an erotic surrealist postcard by the French photographer S.T.A.I., 1930s.

8 Oysters, Sex and Seduction

Think of oysters, think of sex. Myths about the aphrodisiac powers of oysters have proliferated in most cultures for centuries and may have a basis in truth due to the high zinc content of the meat, or may simply be an extension of ancient fertility myths and rituals associated with shells – the word aphrodisiac comes from Aphrodite, goddess of love, born from the sea. The oyster's association with sex is to be taken as read, but what is more interesting is the different *ways* in which oysters have been sexualized in the human imagination and what this tells us about changes in assumptions about sex and sexual behaviour, and indeed gender, in different cultures and different periods of history. For example, the idea in art and literature that oysters increase desire is almost always associated with male arousal and virility, rather than female. Casanova claimed to have eaten as many as sixty oysters a day. The American food writer M.F.K. Fisher wrote in the 1940s: 'there is an astounding number of men, and some of them have graduated from Yale and even Princeton, who know positively that oysters are an aphrodisiac . . . one of the best. They can tell of countless chaps whose powers have been increased nigh unto the billy goat's, simply from eating oysters.'[1]

Oysters are associated with male potency, but they also signify female fertility in many cultures, and have often been given

A T-Shirt equating oysters with Viagra.

c'est si bon

EAT OYSTERS LOVE LONGER

Cajun Viagra

P & J OYSTER COMPANY
New Orleans, Louisiana • 504-529-2151

to girls at puberty or on marriage. They have been linked to other superstitions of gestation and foetal development. Gilbert White, for instance, in *The Natural History of Selbourne* (1778) described a young man who suffered from rough skin: 'The good women, who love to account for every defect in children by the doctrine of longing, said that his mother felt a great propensity for oysters, which she was unable to satisfy, and that the black, rough scurf on his hands and feet were the shells of that fish'. A hundred and fifty years later, the dancer Isadora Duncan playfully claimed a similar explanation for her talent: 'Before I was born my mother was in a great agony of spirit and in a tragic situation. She could take no food except iced oysters and champagne. If people ask me when I began to dance, I reply, "In my mother's womb, probably as a result of the oysters and champagne, the food of Aphrodite."'

Oysters are associated with female sexuality in many complex ways. Throughout the seventeenth and eighteenth centuries, for instance, the woman oyster seller was used in poetry as a figure of erotic play, something, like the oyster, to be consumed, part of the sensuous fruit of the London street for the male urban voyeur. In such descriptions the erotic pleasures of the oyster seem to merge with the figure of the seller herself. In the third book of his *Trivia*, written in 1716, John Gay wrote:

If where Fleet-Ditch with muddy current flows,
You chance to roam, where oyster-tubs in rows
Are rang'd besides the Posts; there stay thy haste,
And with the savoury fish indulge thy taste;
The damsel's knife the gaping shell commands
While the salt liquor streams between her hands.[2]

There are numerous references to oyster-wives and to oyster sellers in seventeenth century writing that show that they were seen as indistinguishable from prostitutes, a commodity on the sexual market. And even in the 1930s a comic sketch on the front cover of the French political and satirical magazine *Le Rire* satirizes this age-old association of prostitutes and showgirls with oysters, as commodities to be consumed by rich older men. Two bored old men converse while showgirls dance before them, their upkicked legs and petticoats transforming them into opened oysters. The caption reads: 'To tell you the truth, these days I'm more excited by a plate of oysters than by a girl's thighs . . .'.

Even in the twentieth century sexual female availability was often symbolized by open oyster-shells. In New Orleans, oyster capital of the United States, Kitty West, cousin of Elvis Presley, performed as Evangeline the Oyster Girl in the 1940s. Her striptease began in an enormous and slowly opened oyster-shell. In Michael Ondaatje's novel of 1979, *Coming Through Slaughter*, the author describes Tom Anderson, 'The King of the District', who every year compiled a Blue Book listing every whore in New Orleans as he would compile a list of local restaurants:

> This was the guide to the sporting district, listing alpha-betically the white and then the black girls, from Martha Alice at 1200 Customhouse to Louisa Walter at 210 North Basin, and the octoroons. The Blue Book and similar guides listed everything, and at any of the mansions you could go in with money and come out broke. No matter how much you took with you, you would lose it all in paying for extras. Such as watching the Oyster Dance – where a naked woman on a small stage danced alone to piano music. The best was Olivia the Oyster Dancer who would place a raw oyster on her forehead and lean back and shimmy it down over her body without ever drop-ping it. The oyster would criss-cross and move finally down to her instep. Then she would kick it high into the air and would catch it on her forehead and begin again.[3]

In the late nineteenth century two of the most notorious pornographic magazines were called *The Oyster* and *The Pearl*, their titles playing provocatively on the notion of purity (the pearl, pearls before swine) and the consumption of flesh (the oyster). But if the oyster is associated with female availability – the flesh to be consumed – a woman eating oysters or breaking open oysters is then perhaps doubly eroticized. In *Lucullus; or, Palatable Essays* (1878), for instance, the anonymous author writes:

'Bored with Showgirls', *Le Rire*, 3 March 1939.

How sweet it is too, to open some of the dear natives for your pretty cousin, and to see her open her sweet little mouth about as wide as Lesbia's sparrow did for his lump of – not sugar, it was not then invented – but lump of honey! How sweet it is, after the young lady has swallowed her half dozen, to help yourself. [4]

The nineteenth-century novelist William Makepeace Thackeray, who found oysters utterly revolting, used the image of a woman eating oysters as the centrepiece of his comic story 'Ottilia' in his adventures of Fitz-boodle to represent the antithesis of desire, revulsion. A beautiful young woman, Ottilia de Schlippenschlopp, has swept the hero off his feet. He is infatuated. The young woman is described as dressed in clothes that suggest the colours, sheens, textures and seductions of an opened oyster as are many of the women oyster-eaters in Dutch seventeenth-century feast scenes:

> Ottilia was pale and delicate. She wore her glistening black hair in bands, and dressed in vapoury white muslin . . . Many is the tea-party I went to, shivering into cold clothes after dinner (which is my abomination), in order to have one little look at the lady of my soul.

The hero begins to have doubts, however, when he sees how much Ottilia eats (though she remains thin). Her gluttony repulses him.

> 'What! Marry,' says I, 'a woman who eats meat twenty-one times a week, besides breakfast and tea? Marry a sarcophagus, a cannibal, a butcher's shop? Away.' I strove and strove. I drank, I groaned, I wrestled and fought with my love – but it overcame me: one look of those eyes brought me to her feet again. I yielded myself up like a slave; I fawned and whined for her . . .

The hero's obsession is only finally broken at the German oyster feast: Fitz-boodle, like Thackeray, finds oysters repulsive and can only eat them well covered in sauces. He also discovers that the oysters on the plate which he and Ottilia are sharing are off. Despite this, Ottilia eats hers voraciously and then turns her

Oyster eaters
afloat.

greedy eyes towards Fitz-boodle's nine uneaten bad oysters
which he incredulously passes to her and watches her eat. 'I left
Kalbsbraten that night', he tells us, 'and have never been there
since.'[5]

When oysters are anthropomorphized they are almost always
male, but when the oyster is eroticized anthropomorphically in
literature then the oyster is usually female. In the mid-nineteenth
century, James Watson Gerard, an American lawyer, judge and
abolitionist, published a series of works in the satirical tradition
of Swift. The first of these, published in 1857, was called
Ostrea; or, The Loves of the Oysters and was dedicated to male epicures: 'my grinding, gulping, gorging, stuffing, tucking, bolting
Brobdingnagians . . . my Flagellators of the Flesh-pots'. The book
is a series of mock-heroic poems in which oysters are anthropomorphized and eroticized as star-crossed lovers, doomed to
destruction by the greed of man. The first poem introduces the
oyster with direct reference to the most erotic and controversial

poems published in nineteenth-century America, *Leaves of Grass*, published only two years earlier in 1855 by Walt Whitman. One of the most notorious poems in that collection begins 'I sing the body electric'. Gerard begins with a male oyster:

I sing the Oyster! (Virgin Theme!)
King of Molluscules! Ancient of the stream!

But then Mya is introduced, the poem's oyster heroine, both object and subject of desire:

Mya! – fairest of shell-fish, she
That creep the shore, or swim the sea,
Or haunt the slimy ooze; –
Oyster of ancient family,
Of tender years, scarce summers three
Her rounded valves disclose [. . .]
With softest yellow shines her skin,
While violet blood, her veins within,
Reveals a purple hue.
Polished each shell on outward side,
By amorous kissings of the tide
Long loving and caressing.

This beautiful oyster of ancient family mourns her lost love Loligo (which means squid) who has gone to sea but who eventually returns to be 'clasped within her shell'. The two are married, like Romeo and Juliet, in a secret cave:

By altar of rosy coral placed,
Tenderly with shell inlaced,
The twain became but one:

No witnesses, save crickets three,
Who, passing, stop and sing with glee
Their epithalamium

And now by Hymen's fetters tied,
Loligo bears his juicy bride
Beneath the sparkling flood;
There wrapped in bliss, the happy pair
The honeymoon together share,
In softest Jersey mud!

The final poem in the sequence is another mock-heroic poem about man's greed and cruelty to animals. Long clusters of stanzas turn on the thoughts of the oyster lovers, now caught, dragged up from their seabed and condemned to death, as the cooking pot heats up.

Together STEWED! Within the pot they lie! –
Mourn ye fond lovers! Their untimely fate,
Weep, weep, ye cupids who on lovers wait –
Yet – weep them not, nor mourn their early doom
In Julia's throat! They find an envied tomb![6]

The poem is a wonderfully satirical play on cultures of eating and sex so that it becomes difficult to tell where flesh begins and ends. Mya enfolds Loligo, the two are joined, then both cooked and eaten – their final resting place in the throat of Julia. Insides and outsides, flesh inside flesh.

But although oysters have been used for centuries as a nudge-nudge euphemism for sexually available female flesh, writers from as early as the eighteenth and nineteenth centuries tell counter-stories of women who, like Daniel Defoe's Moll in

Moll Flanders (1722) or like Lizzie in Christina Rossetti's 'Goblin Market' (1862), are able to work the sexual market to their own advantage. Rather than represented simply as commodities, like oysters themselves, to be consumed, flesh for the taking, they begin to be the subjects of their own sexuality, able to define their own deals in the exchange of money for sex in the sexual market. Here, for instance, is a Victorian broadside:

As I was going down Bishopgate-street,
An oyster girl I chanced to meet,
Into her basket I chanced to peep,
To see if she had any oysters.

Oysters, oysters, oysters, sir, said she,
They are the best you e'er did see,
And if you please to buy them of me,
I'll warrant 'em all fat oysters.

And if to a tavern you'll go with me,
With a bottle of wine I'll treat thee,
And all so merrily we'll agree,
With bread and wine to our oysters.

They had not long at the tavern been,
When she picked his pocket of four-score pounds,
She gave him the slip and ran into town,
Thus dearly he paid for his oysters.

O waiter, waiter, did you see,
An oyster girl come in with me?
She's picked my pocket of all my money,
And left me her basket of oysters.

O yes, kind sir, I did see
An oyster girl come in with thee,
She paid the reck'ning – so you may go free,
And troop with your basket of oysters.

Of all the years I lived in France,
I never met with such a mischance,
An oyster girl gave to me a fine dance
And made me pay dear for my oysters.

Nancy, the heroine of Sarah Waters's novel *Tipping the Velvet* (1999) is another example of a streetwise sexual adventurer. She tells us that she grew up in her father's seaside restaurant, shucking oysters and stirring soup: 'Although I didn't believe the story told to me by Mother – that they had found me as a baby in an oyster-shell, and a greedy customer had almost eaten me for lunch – for 18 years I never doubted my own oysterish sympathies . . . '.[7] When she visits the local music hall at night and sees a male impersonator, her life of sexual transformations begins. Her oysterish upbringing and the constant references to her oyster childhood in the novel are a perfect counterpoint to the sexual ambiguity and fluidity of the oyster itself, able to be both male and female by turns, as if by will. Whilst the lifecycle of the oyster might have offered a metaphor of the naturalness of settling down for the Victorians, for Sarah Waters it is a metaphor of sexual fluidity and bisexuality. Nancy turns and turns, performs her male/female sexuality in music halls, in alleyways, in drawing rooms and brothels.

Oysters have also been used in film and in fiction as a way of signalling homosexual desire. In an extraordinary story published in the *Harmondsworth Magazine* in August 1899 a shared oyster passion is the occasion for a scene of homosexual innuendo of the most elaborate and transparent kind. The plot is a simple one: an impoverished actor and painter with epicurean tastes hatch a plot to enable them to eat fresh oysters regularly. In the local oyster restaurant the actor slips a small seed pearl into one of his oysters and claims to have found it there. The restaurateur is embarrassed, but the story quickly brings in many more customers all ordering oysters in the hope that they too will find pearls. The two men return to confess to the fraud and threaten to take the true story to the newspapers unless the restaurateur agrees to feed them unlimited oysters once a week. The owner reluctantly agrees.

The story may be simple enough but the sexual innuendo is not. Take the scene in which the two men discover their mutual passion for oysters. The actor confesses to his 'sin' with his legs tilted upwards 'optimistically' in the air; 'emboldened by his confidences' the painter also confesses and clasps his friend's hand. In fact there is a good deal of passionate hand clasping in this scene as the painter declares that the two of them are 'in love' and the actor proposes that they seal their friendship with an oyster carnival.

> On one of these occasions he confessed to me his besetting sin. It took the form of an unholy and ravenous craving for – oysters. Seated in his favourite attitude (with legs tilted optimistically upwards, to assist thought by directing the flow of blood to the brain) he expounded his reasons and desires at length . . . 'Give me, sir, the oyster *au naturel*, coy and disdainful in its close-clasped, pearly shell, oh my boy!'
>
> Inspired by his glowing description, emboldened by his confidences, I arose and clasped his hand, whilst in a

choking voice I explained that he had discovered the secret sorrow of my soul – the lack of oysters in an impecunious world. He apologised for intruding on my grief, and then we sat in silence to ruminate upon the joy of meeting a kindred spirit, a friend capable of great appreciation. Into our hearts then stole the pleasure that men feel when in love, but without the deterioration of intellect consequent upon that condition.

At length some ashes fell with a tiny crash into the grate and awoke us from our reveries. This time it was Tom who extended his hand. 'Come' he cried. 'Let us seal the bond of eternal friendship with an oyster carnival! Come!'[8]

Sixty years later oysters were censored by Universal Studios from the famous bathroom scene between Laurence Olivier and Tony Curtis in Stanley Kubrick's *Spartacus*. Universal Studios felt that this scene, in which Crassus attempts to seduce Antonius by telling him that he likes both snails and oysters, was too sexually explicit. The scene was only restored in 1990.

One of the most interesting uses of the oyster is in accounts of sexual rites of passage, in which a pubescent child passes through a sexual or sexually charged encounter, to become an adult. In a poem by Anne Sexton, for instance, called 'Death of the Fathers, 1. Oysters', published in *The Book of Folly* in 1972, the speaker records her metamorphosis from girl to woman in a restaurant in which her father watches her eat oysters:

> Oysters we ate,
> sweet blue babies,
> twelve eyes looked up at me,
> running with lemon and Tabasco.
> I was afraid to eat this father-food

and Father laughed and drank down his martini,
clear as tears.
It was a soft medicine
that came from the sea into my mouth,
moist and plump.
I swallowed.
It went down like a large pudding.
Then I ate one o'clock and two o'clock.
Then I laughed and then we laughed
and let me take note –
there was a death,
the death of childhood
there at the Union Oyster House
for I was fifteen
and eating oysters
and the child was defeated.
The woman won.

In *Kitchen Confidential*, Anthony Bourdain tells a similar story to that of Anne Sexton and to that of Hector Bolitho in *The Glorious Oyster*. He too performs this act of eating raw flesh in the sight of his parents as an act of defiance, a 'death': 'Now, this was a truly significant event. I remember it like I remember losing my virginity – and in many ways, more fondly.' Bourdain was staying in a tiny oyster village on the Bassin d'Arcachon in south-west France. When the local oyster fisherman took Bourdain's American family out to see the oyster-beds, he asked if any of them would like to try an oyster:

My parents hesitated. I doubt they'd realised they might actually have to eat one of the raw, slimy things we were currently floating over. My little brother recoiled in horror.

But I, in the proudest moment of my young life, stood up smartly, grinning with defiance, and volunteered to be the first.

And in that unforgettably sweet moment in my personal history, that one moment still more alive for me than so many of the other 'firsts' that followed – first pussy, first joint, first day in high school, first published book, or any other thing – I attained glory . . . With a snubby, rust-covered knife [Monsieur Saint-Jour] popped the thing open and handed it to me, everyone watching now, my little brother shrinking away from this glistening, vaguely sexual-looking object, still dripping and nearly alive.

I took it in my hand, tilted the shell back to my mouth as instructed by the now beaming Monsieur Saint-Jour,

Osias Beert the Elder, *Still-life with Oysters*, 1610, oil on copper.

and with one bite and a slurp, wolfed it down. It tasted of seawater . . . of brine and flesh... and somehow . . . of the future.

Everything was different now. Everything.

. . . I'd learned something. Viscerally, instinctively, spiritually – even in some small, precursive way, sexually – and there was no turning back. The genie was out of the bottle. My life as a cook and as a chef, had begun.

Food had power.[9]

Oysters when sexualized, in the hands of writers, photographers, artists and film-makers swing all ways. Oysters themselves swing all ways – male and female by turns, sexually fluid, hugely fertile. To humankind they have spoken – and continue to speak – of desire and unappeasable hunger and of flesh to be consumed. Do oysters enhance sexual prowess? Well, if they don't do so chemically, they certainly do so by their age-old cultural associations with flesh, hunger and intimacy. Think of oysters, try *not* to think of sex.

9 Pearl

In Jan Vermeer's haunting oil painting of 1665, *Girl with a Pearl Earring*, a beautiful young woman turns towards us, her wet mouth slightly open as if she has been hailed in the act of daydreaming or as if she is about to speak. For a moment time has stopped, yet the veil from her turban appears to be still moving in that unseen turn towards us, and the pearl suspended from her ear seems to sway still. Her gaze is unnerving, disturbingly intimate, but she looks at the same time vulnerable, poised and very young. The light catches her pearl earring, the whites of her eyes, the sheen of her skin and the glow of her white linen collar, all the more iridescent for the painting's midnight-black background.

Jan Vermeer loved pearls as Osias Beert loved oyster flesh, but though pearls are produced by oysters, they rarely appear together in Western art. Pearl earrings appear on women in seven of Vermeer's other canvases all painted from the mid-1660s onwards, the same decade in which Beert was painting his oysters: *Woman with a Pearl Necklace, Woman with a Lute, The Concert, A Lady Writing, Girl with a Red Hat, A Study of a Young Woman, Mistress and her Maid* and *Lady Writing a Letter with her Maid*. For Beert and Vermeer the whites of wet oyster flesh, of mother-of-pearl and of pearls were never *just* 'white' – they provided a tonal range and a play of light never to be entirely caught

Jan Vermeer, *Girl with a Pearl Earring*, 1665, oil on canvas.

or mastered. And the meanings of oysters and pearls were as multiple and illusive as their whitenesses. If the oyster spoke of both shell-embodied timelessness and fleshly transience, of vanity, desire and intimacy, the pearl too contained multitudes of meanings: it spoke of innocence and of vanity but, more than anything, it spoke of wealth. A year after Vermeer painted *Girl with a Pearl Earring*, the English diarist Samuel Pepys purchased a single pearl for £80, worth £7,500 today.[1] Across the world, pearls were traded, fought over, treasured, painted, set in elaborate necklaces or in the velvet, silk and satin of

A pearl in an oyster.

Pearls for sale in China.

dresses and shoes. Pearls made fortunes and lost others; they shaped the lines and trade routes of empires. By the time Vermeer painted this exquisite painting, scores of thousands of enslaved pearl-divers had been cruelly worked to their death in the pearl fisheries of the Spanish empire.

The pearl is a miracle of evolutionary processes, for it is the only gem produced by a living animal. Long ago certain molluscs evolved a way of protecting their soft flesh from their rough shell by secreting nacre or mother-of-pearl as a perfectly smooth lining to their shells. A smaller group of molluscs then evolved a way of dealing with the tearing caused by grits of sand or the burrowings of parasitic worms – these too could be coated with white nacre. So the iridescent whiteness of pearls is formed deep in mollusc flesh by layered mother-of-pearl secretions – a mixture of calcium carbonate and an animal substance called conchiolin. The finest pearls come from a branch of the oyster family called *Meleagrina margaritifera* and take about three years to reach full size, layer upon nacreous layer. Pearls are then, in the words of M.F.K. Fisher, 'gleaming "worm-coffins" . . . built in what may be pain around the bodies that have crept inside the shells'.[2] And in the mid-nineteenth century another natural history writer mused: 'It is a singular reflection that the gem so admired and coveted by man should be the product of disease in a helpless mollusk.'[3]

Pearl oysters grow in a remarkable range of habitats. Freshwater species grow in the rivers and lakes of China, Great Britain, Europe and North America. Saltwater species grow on the shorelines of the Pacific islands, the Red Sea, the Indian Ocean, the Persian Gulf, along the Atlantic and Pacific coasts of Central America, the Gulf of Mexico and the Caribbean, among the islands of the English Channel and in the waters of the Arabian Sea. But although pearl oysters grow almost everywhere, they produce pearls under natural conditions only very rarely. In 1947, for example, only 21 pearls were found in 35,000 Persian Gulf oysters. Most are very small and are called seed pearls. Pearl fishing is thus very labour intensive.

No two pearls are the same for each is made from the mother-of-pearl lining produced by a particular oyster in a particular place. Mother-of-pearl can be pink, rose, white, yellow, cream, golden, green, blue and black. The finest pink and cream coloured oysters are produced by a small pearl oyster called *Margaritifera vulgaris* native to the Persian Gulf. Large silver-white pearls called silver-lips are found in the northern waters of Australia. Black pearls come from the South Seas.

The shape of the pearl, which also affects its price, depends on how it grows inside the shell. Pearls that grow without pressure assume a pear shape; those that grow within muscular tissue will assume an irregular shape; those that grow attached to the shell will grow into a half-sphere and be flattened on one side. These are called blister, mabe or button pearls. And pearls can be shaped too by human hand. Mary Fisher describes seeing pearl talismans on the markets of Soochow in China that had been made by the insertion of small moulded objects such as phalluses and Buddhas into pearl oysters.

Pearl fishers from a manuscript of 1338, Marco Polo's *Les Livres du Graut Caam.*

As pearls appear in Indian culture very early, they were probably first discovered by the Dravidian fishermen of southern India when they were fishing for oysters. Pearl necklaces are described in the great Hindu religious poem, the *Ramayana*, written about 500 BC. When Marco Polo visited these coasts on his return voyage from China in 1293, he described a long-established and elaborate pearl fishing trade: 'pearls are fished in great quantities, for thence come the pearls which are spread all over the world'.[4] Phoenician traders from the eastern Mediterranean carried pearls back from India to ancient Greece. When the Romans conquered Greece, Egypt, Mesopotamia and Persia, pearls became one of the most important gems in the Roman currency system. The pearl trade had begun and its story would be one of decimation, enslavement and exploitation as well as flamboyant sartorial beauty.

The pearl oyster has kept its evolutionary secret for millions of years. Davidian, Persian, Bahrainian and Chinese fishermen may have had their own understandings of pearl formation, but the naturalists and mythologists of ancient India, Greece and Rome believed that pearls were formed when oysters rose to the surface of the sea, opened their valves to capture drops of rain or dew and then returned to the sea bed to transform dew into pearls. The ancient Chinese held that pearls were the tears of dragons, sharks or mermaids. In his *Natural History* completed in AD 77, Pliny the Elder wrote confidently that oysters,

> when stimulated by the generative season of the year gape open as it were and are filled with dewy pregnancy, and subsequently when heavy are delivered, and the offspring of the shells are pearls that correspond to the quality of the dew received; if it was a pure inflow, their brilliance is conspicuous, but if it was turbid, the product becomes dirty in colour.[5]

As a consequence of these myths, tears and lamentation have come to be entangled with the cultural meanings of pearls. When John Webster's persecuted duchess, for instance, in *The Duchess of Malfi* (written 1612–13; published 1623) tells her husband Antonio about her strange dream, she says: 'Methought I wore my coronet of state, And on a sudden all the diamonds Were chang'd to pearls'; Antonio replies: 'My interpretation Is, you'll weep shortly; for to me the pearls Do signify your tears.' (Act III, scene v). The duchess's pearl dream-tears are poignantly prophetic – she and her young children are imprisoned and then strangled only a few days later.

This theory of the pearl's dewy origin persisted until the eighteenth century, when scientists began to study the formation of pearls with the use of microscopes. In the eighteenth century the Swedish naturalist Carl Linnaeus experimented with the artificial production of pearls by inserting foreign bodies into their shells. In a letter to the Swiss anatomist, Von Haller, dated 13 September 1748, he wrote: 'At length I have ascertained the manner in which pearls originate and grow in shells; and in the course of five or six years I am able to produce, in my mother-of-pearl shell the size of one's hand, a pearl as large as the seed of the common vetch.'[6] By the nineteenth century most scientists had come to agree that pearls formed in response to the presence of an irritant, but the pearl's cultural association with tears and dew-drops persisted. Sir Edward Arnold, English poet and translator of Sanskrit texts, for instance, wrote about pearls in the late nineteenth century as an emblem of stoicism:

> Know you, perchance how that poor formless wretch –
> The oyster – gems his shallow moonlit chalice?
> Where the shell irks him, or the sea-sand frets,
> He sheds this lovely lustre on his grief.

But the pearl has also signified transformation from a lowly state to a holy one – the exquisite pearl formed within lowly oyster flesh. Early Christians used the pearl as a metaphor for the virgin birth of Christ or for the divine soul housed within the earthly body. As early as the thirteenth century a Persian poet, Sa'di, wrote in his *Bustan* ('Fruit Garden') an exquisite parable of transmigration:

A drop of water fell one day from a cloud into the sea. Ashamed and confounded on finding itself in such an immensity of water, it exclaimed, 'What am I in comparison with this vast ocean? My existence is less than nothing in this boundless abyss.' Whilst it thus discoursed of itself, a Pearl-Shell received it into his bosom, and fortune so favoured it, that it became a magnificent and

James Herbert Draper, *A Water Baby*, 1900, oil on canvas.

precious pearl, worthy of adorning the diadem of kings. Thus was its humility the cause of its elevation, and by annihilating itself it merited exaltation.[7]

In one of Shakespeare's late plays of transformation and redemption a drowned king's tears are turned into pearls: in *The Tempest* (1610–11), Ariel describes Ferdinand's dead father in a song:

Full fathom five thy father lies;
Of his bones are coral made;
Those are pearls that were his eyes:
Nothing of him that doth fade
But doth suffer a sea-change
Into something rich and strange.

In 1839 the Christian poet and hymn writer James Montgomery joined both Sa'di and Shakespearean sources in a poem about the meeting of soul and body through Christ called 'Transmigrations':

A hailstone, from the cloud set free,
Shot, slanting coastward, o'er the sea,
And thus, as eastern tales relate,
Lamented its untimely fate:
'Last moment born, condemned in this,
The next absorbt in yon abyss;
'Twere better ne're to know the light,
Than see and perish at first sight.'

An oyster heard, and, as it fell,
Welcomed the outcast to her shell,

Where, meekly suffering that 'sea-change'
It grew to 'something rich and strange',
And thence became the brightest gem
That decks the Sultan's diadem,
Turned from a particle of ice
Into a pearl of priceless price

Thus can the power that rules o'er all
Exalt the humble by their fall.[8]

So if the myths of pearl origins conjoin suffering and lamentation with great value, so too does the history of man's use of pearls – a history of wealth made by one group of people through the exploitation and suffering of others.

PEARLS AND EMPIRE

Shakespeare's famous lines from *Troilus and Cressida* (written *c.* 1602; first printed 1609) describe Helen of Troy as:

... the pearl
Whose price hath launched a thousand ships
And turned crown'd kings to merchants. (Act II, scene iii)

Helen, like the pearl, Shakespeare implies, has a beauty that is dangerous in a world dominated by greed and the desire to possess. It is only to be gained at a high price and – at worst – with considerable loss of life, for Helen's beauty, like that of the pearl, was traded, negotiated and fought over.

Pearls have drawn the lines and borders of empires. Most of the great ancient civilizations were located near the richest pearl fisheries across Persia, the Red Sea and the Indian Ocean.

The Persian Gulf became one of the first trading centres for pearls in the first centuries BC, and, after its assimilation by Islam in the seventh century, the Persian court became one of the most opulent in the world. European tales and myths proliferated concerning the fabulous riches of the East. As trade routes developed outwards from the Persian Gulf, pearls were carried from East to West and, for Western poets, painters and writers became a potent symbol for the presumed mystery, wealth and beauty of the East.

The Romans developed a passion for pearls as they had for oysters. Because they were rare and beautiful but also extremely costly, the Romans used pearls in jewellery as a visible marker of status and wealth, a show of conspicuous consumption. Seneca, the statesman, philosopher and dramatist, wrote disparagingly of the taste for pearl earrings in Rome: 'Simply one for each ear? No! The lobes of our ladies have attained a special capacity for supporting a great number . . . they wear the value of an inheritance in each ear'.[9]

According to Pliny, Cleopatra, the Egyptian queen who ruled from 51 to 30 BC, performed one of the most spectacular acts of conspicuous consumption in human history. In a dramatic and erotically charged meeting of East and West, she entertained the Roman senator Mark Antony with lavish banquets in order to impress on him the wealth and beauty of Egypt. At one of these she wagered with him that she could consume the wealth of a single country in one meal. Antony accepted the wager, but when he arrived for dinner the following evening he found that the banquet was no more sumptuous than usual. After dinner, Cleopatra removed a large pearl from one of her earrings, crushed it, stirred the powder into her wine and drank it. Pliny estimated the value of that single pearl to have been the equivalent of a million ounces of silver.

But the value of the pearl in Western culture reached its zenith in that great era of conspicuous consumption: the Renaissance. In 1498 Christopher Columbus 'discovered' the three major islands off the eastern coast of Venezuela: Coche, Cubagua and Margarita. Trading with the natives he discovered they were adorned with gold and pearls. 'Seeing this I was much delighted', he wrote.[10] But it was the Spanish who returned the following year to claim these islands for the Spanish crown and to name the region the Costa de las Perlas. The pearl rush was now on. For decades, pearls were a more prized commodity than gold, as the ruling families of Europe – the Habsburgs, the Valois of France, the Medici and Borgia of Italy, the Tudors and Stuarts of England – sent their agents to bid for the largest pearls available from the pearl-trading merchants as their boats returned from Persia and India.

George Morrow, 'Marginal Notes on History. Family Physician (to Cleopatra). "AH! WE'VE BEEN DRINKING PEARLS AGAIN, HAVE WE?"', an illustration from *Punch* (28 February 1912).

With the increasing demand for pearls in Europe, the Spanish tried to increase their supply from the Pearl Coast. In the early years of the trade the Spanish pearl merchants employed the natives from Margarita to dive for pearls and paid for them in wine, linen shirts, wheat bread, firearms and other European goods. But when the Guayquer started to raise their prices, tensions arose. The Spanish were in a difficult position – none of them could swim, let alone dive to the pearl beds that were between 13 and 22 metres deep – so they began to import slave labourers from surrounding islands, including the indigenous peoples of Trinidad and the Venezuelan mainland coast and large numbers of Lucayan Indians from the Bahamas, who were especially prized for their swimming skills and deep-diving abilities. A young Lucayan diver fetched 150 gold pesos (ducats) in the slave market in the early decades of the sixteenth century, equivalent to about £35 today. Within ten years, the Bahamas had been completely depopulated of Lucayos from an original population believed to be 60,000 people. All for pearls.

Enslaved pearl divers were treated harshly. Branded on the face and arms and whipped if they rested for too long between dives, they were chained at night and forced to dive throughout the daylight hours. Sharks killed many divers; others died from haemorrhages produced by water pressure or intestinal disorders caused by diving in cold water. There was much at stake: a single boat could harvest 35,000 oysters in two weeks.

By the 1520s Cubagua, an island only 8.5 square miles in diameter, had became a wild mining 'frontier' land with a resident population of nearly 300. Drinking, gambling, murder, adultery and the rape of native women were common. Punishment of insurrection amongst the natives had become both ritualistic and sadistic. The slave divers, now desperate and with little to lose, ambushed and massacred a notoriously cruel slaver and his men, burned the missions on the mainland, killing all the friars, and poisoned the water springs in Margarita. When a newly arrived ship came ashore, the pearl divers axed the crew to death and took the ships. Under siege and with no fresh water, the Spanish settlers seized 200 Margarita natives who were expert divers, crammed them into four ships and returned to Hispaniola. From there the government sent a large force to crush the rebellion and to build a fortress at Nueva Cadiz on Margarita, which, in 1527, became the first European city in South America.

Now with a good deal of money invested in the Pearl Coast from which he demanded a return in jewels, the Spanish king authorized the use of dredges, although local people warned that dredging would severely deplete the oyster-beds. They were right: by 1531 the pearl supply was beginning to decline, and although the Spanish began to place limits on boat size, on the number of divers per boat and the number of diving hours, within five years there were no pearls left in the Cubaguan beds. The colonists moved out, taking the slave divers with them; by 1539 there were between 10 and 50 people left on the island. On Christmas Day 1541 a hurricane and tidal wave destroyed the remaining buildings and wiped out the last occupants. Cubagua was never permanently inhabited again.

When the French essayist Michel de Montaigne read Francisco López de Gómara's *Historia General de las Indias* (1552), he was appalled at the greed and decimation the pearl trade had excited: 'So many goodly cities ransacked and razed; so many nations destroyed and made desolate; . . . the richest, the fairest and the best part of the world topsiturvied, ruined and defaced for the traffick of Pearles and Pepper'.[11] Once the supply of riches from the Americas had been depleted, the Spanish economy did not recover. In a decade or so, in search of

quick wealth, the Spanish had decimated the native popula-
tions used as slave divers along the Pearl Coast and created one
of the fastest cases of natural resource depletion in history,
leaving behind them the empty shell of a colony built for the
production of wealth.

Few consumers of pearls in the sixteenth century knew the
horrors of the pearl coast. If they had known about the conditions of the divers, however, it is still unlikely that pearls might
have been boycotted as fur is by certain groups today. Elizabeth I,
who ruled England from 1558 until her death in 1603, was, like
Cleopatra, a mistress of spectacle and conspicuous display; like
Cleopatra she used the pearl as a centrepiece in the composition
of her public image. She was rarely seen or painted without
them. The eighteenth-century art collector Horace Walpole
described Elizabeth's astutely iconographic self-representation:
'A pale Roman nose, a head of hair loaded with crowns and
powdered with diamonds, a vast ruff, a vaster fardingdale, and
a bushel of pearls, are the features by which everybody knows at
once the pictures of Elizabeth I.'

In an age of emblems, pearls signified a queen's purity and
chastity as well as immortality. Even Elizabeth's pet ermine is
shown in one portrait wearing a pearl-encrusted collar. Sir
Francis Bacon suggested that the queen's pearl- and jewel-
encrusted public image also served to distract attention away
from the fact of her aging (her increasingly thick white face
paint could not disguise this): 'she imagined that the people,
who are much influenced by externals, would be diverted by
the glitter of her jewels, from noticing the decay of her personal attractions'. At her funeral Elizabeth's coffin bore her wax
effigy dressed in wax facsimiles of her pearls: a coronet of large
spherical pearls, pearl earrings and pearl medallions on her
shoe-bows. A poet at the time wrote that as the funeral proces-

Anonymous, *Coronation Portrait of Elizabeth I*, 1600, oil on canvas.

sion passed along the River Thames, 'Fish wept their eyes of pearl quite out / And swam blind after'.[12]

The Pearl Age came to an end in the seventeenth century with political turmoil, the Thirty Years War, Protestant uprisings and the growth of a new aesthetic of austerity in Protestant Europe. By the mid-eighteenth century most of the natural pearl fisheries around the world had been fished to exhaustion,

Pearl head-dresses
worn in Russia in
the seventeenth
century.

but nonetheless, perhaps because of the natural pearl's rarity, pearls rose in popularity again, particularly among the royal families of Europe. Aristocratic women wore pearl parures – matched sets of necklaces, bracelets, earrings and brooches. Pearls were particularly popular in Russia in the eighteenth century, worn in elaborately patterned head-dresses.

The Jewesses of Little Russia also had a tradition of wearing pearl-caps in the mid-nineteenth century, as the German traveller Johann Georg Kohl described in 1846:

For all the women through South and Little Russia and even as far as Galicia wear a certain stiff, baggy cap which is very disfiguring, and is covered all over with a great number of pearls, upon a foundation of black velvet. It is called a 'mushka' . . . They spend their last money in order to secure such a pearl-cap and even when they are clad in rags their head is covered with pearls. In order to furnish the requisite material for this wide-spread fashion, the commerce in pearls of Odessa, Taganrog and some other places in Southern Russia is not unimportant. There may live in the regions where the pearl caps of which I speak are worn at least 2,000,000 Jewesses . . . We inquired of our beautiful Jewess whether she was not in perpetual dread on account of her pearl-cap, and how she protected it from thieves. She answered that she wore it on her head all day and at night placed it in a casket which rested under the pillow. So that the whole short life of these Jewesses of the steppes revolves around their pearl-cap as the earth does around the sun.[13]

Russian refugees from the Bolshevik Revolution who migrated to Paris in the 1920s brought with them these Russian traditions of pearl ornamentation, and created a new European taste for Czarist jewellery, relics and *objets d'art*. In 1910, just before the outbreak of the First World War, the Ballets Russes' production of Diaghilev's *Scheherezade* (Paris, 1910) caused a sensation in Paris and influenced new fashions in dress and interior decor. The Ballets Russes' co-founder and costume and stage designer was Léon Bakst, a Jewish Belorussian who designed exotic, orientalized pearl-studded costumes in canary yellows, bright blues, jades, cyclamens, hennas and reds dramatically contrasted against backgrounds of black, deep green and tobacco browns.

Rudolph Valentino dressed in pearls for the film *The Young Rajah*, 1922.

opposite:
In 1927 the designer Judith Barbier introduced this crocheted headpiece designed to resemble the pearl headdresses popular in the fourteenth century.

In 1912, exiled as a Jew from St Petersberg, Bakst settled in Paris. The fashion designer Paul Poiret (1880–1944), influenced by Bakst's new exotic orientalism, created turbans and minaret skirts covered with cultured pearls. Another Russian designer, born Romain de Tirtoff but who called himself Erté after the French pronunciation of his own initials, started producing whimsical clothing designs covered in pearls as well as pearl-studded costumes for the Folies Bergère. At the same time the extraordinary African-American dancer Josephine Baker arrived sensationally on the Parisian stage, her beautiful muscular body often only adorned by feathers or strings of cultured pearls.

By the latter part of the twentieth century only the very rich – or the glamorous recipients of gifts from the very rich, like Grace Kelly and Audrey Hepburn – could afford natural pearls. Richard Burton bought the famous pear-shaped La Peregrina pearl for Elizabeth Taylor in 1969, which was believed to have been discovered near Panama in the sixteenth century by a slave diver who bought his liberty with it. The pearl was sent to Spain and presented to Philip II and later given as a wedding gift to Mary Tudor when she married Philip. Elizabeth Taylor famously lost it at a casino. After a frantic search the pearl was found in the mouth of her pet dog.

PEARL DIVING

Local people were fishing for pearls in the Persian Gulf as long ago as the second millennium BC. A cuneiform inscription from the ancient Assyrian city of Ninevah describes a king's interest in 'the sea of changeable winds' where 'his merchants fished for pearls'.[14] Methods of diving for oysters have changed very little throughout the centuries. In the South Seas and in Japan most pearl divers have been women. In the Persian Gulf and the waters of Ceylon and India most have been men. Since the end of the enslavement of the pearl divers, these men and women have inspired enormous respect from their own tribes and communities for the skill, courage and risks they undertook.

In the Persian Gulf the pearl season has for centuries lasted from June until early October. Small boats with a captain, several divers and attendants sailed out of the harbour in three or four fleets; these pearl divers were usually migrant workers arriving at the coast just before the season began and returning to their homes when it was over. Until recently, most wore only a loin-cloth, a horn nose-clip and finger thimbles to protect their hands.

Bahrainian pearl divers in the Persian Gulf wearing noseclips.

They stepped into the loop of a rope attached to a rock or iron weight and jumped into the water, sinking quickly to the bottom. A second rope had a basket attached to it to hold the oysters. When the basket was full, which would take about a minute, the diver pulled on the rope to be pulled back up with his basket. On the boat he rested for two or three minutes, before diving again, making 40 or 50 dives a day throughout the four-month season. On shore, other migrant workers searched the oysters for pearls, kneading through piles of oyster flesh. Then shell and oyster meat would be thrown overboard.

In Japan, pearl divers – or *ama* – have been girls or women for centuries, frequently depicted by Japanese printmakers in the eighteenth and nineteenth centuries sitting on the edge of the land, feet in the water, half-dressed, working, feeding their children, wringing out their loincloths, searching through opened oyster-shells or combing their hair, sublimely unaware of the gaze fixed on them. As early as the eighth century the poet Lady Nakatomi described their skills and courage:

Utamaro, *Abalone Divers*, centre-piece of 19th-century triptych, woodblock print.

No one dives to the ocean-bottom
Just like that.
One does not learn the skills involved
At the drop of a hat.
It's the slow-learnt skills in the depths of love
That I am working at.

The *ama* have been romanticized as mermaids but the demands of the pearl trade have meant that they rarely rest during the daylight hours. These women inhabit 24 villages

The female pearl divers of Japan, known as *ama*.

on the coastline of Japan and dive as deep as 60 feet (18 metres) wearing nothing but loincloths, sounding the *ama-bui* whistle as they surface. Photographs of the semi-naked women show the strength and muscularity of their limbs. When the Pearl King Mikimoto employed these *ama* in the twentieth century in his cultured pearl beds, he instituted a new dress code, replacing the loincloths with white cotton garments that covered them from neck to knees, for safety reasons.

For centuries pearls have drawn the lines of empires and, where pearl divers have been enslaved, the pearl trade has decimated communities and destroyed cultures. But if the pearl trade has broken up communities, it has made other, strangely itinerant multi-cultural communities on shorelines around the world, brought together for a few months for pearl harvesting. In 1908,

for instance, George Frederick Kunz described the opening of the pearl-fishing season in Marichchikadde in India, describing the pearl harvesting as a kind of Babel, as men, women and children from all parts of the East gathered not just for the pearl harvest but also for its market, a shoreline city built on and for pearls:

opposite:
Fosco Maraini,
'Diving *ama*',
from *L'Isola delle pescatrici*, Bari,
1960.

A week or so before the opening of the season the boats begin to arrive, sometimes fifty or more in a single day, laden with men, women and children, and in many cases with the materials for their huts. In a short time the erstwhile desolate beach becomes populated with thousands of persons from all over the Indian littoral, and there is the noisy traffic of congregated humanity, and a confusion of tongues where before only the sound of the ocean waves was heard. Beside the eight or ten thousand fishermen, most of whom are Moormen, Tamils and Arabs, there are pearl merchants – mainly Chetties and Moormen, boat repairers and other mechanics, provision dealers, priests, pawnbrokers, government officials, koddu-counters, clerks, boat guards, a police force of 200 officials, coolies, domestic servants, with numbers of women and children. And for the entertainment of these, and to obtain a share of the wealth from the sea, there are jugglers, fakirs, gamblers, beggars, female dancers, loose characters, with every allurement that appeals to the sons of Brahma, Buddha or Mohammed. Natives from the seaport towns of India are there in thousands; the slender-limbed and delicate-featured Cingalese with their scant attire and unique head-dress; energetic Arabs from the Persian Gulf; burly Moormen, sturdy Kandyans, outcast Veddahs, Chinese, Jews, Portuguese, Dutch, half-castes, the scum of the East and the riffraff of the Asiatic littoral, the whole making up a temporary city of forty or more inhabitants.[15]

If a drop in market price had turned oysters into the food of the poor in the nineteenth century due to developments in oyster farming and transportation, the pearl, as an adornment of clothing, also changed its status at around the same time. For scores of centuries pearls have been worn by the rich and powerful and have – all too often – resulted in the exploitation of the weak. Along with gold and diamonds, they have been one of the principal markers of conspicuous consumption. But in the nineteenth century, mass-production techniques of pearl buttons enabled by the Industrial Revolution made it possible for the very poor to mimic and even subvert the use of the pearl as a marker of wealth. Pearl buttons, carved out of the mother-of-pearl lining of oyster-shells by new cutting machines, were striking but relatively cheap to produce. In the second half of the nineteenth century pearl button makers flourished in Britain and America. In *Silver-Shell; or, the Adventures of an Oyster* (1856), the Revd Charles Williams describes the manufacture of pearl buttons in Birmingham in the mid-nineteenth century. Huge storerooms on the Birmingham docks housed piles of oyster-shells from the coasts of Ceylon and from the Australian seas. Merchants bought them for £120 per ton.

> Let us now transport ourselves to one of the large manufactories of Birmingham. Ascending the stairs and entering a room, we see some shells washed in water and we follow a basket of them to witness the operation of another department. A man stands here at a strongly formed

lathe, which, revolving, puts in motion, a hollow spindle,
having at one end some saw-like teeth, presses the shell
against the teeth to cut it into circular piles.[16]

The Revd Williams then describes how women engravers
impress the shapes of rings, stars, foxes, fishes and greyhounds,
for instance, on to the pearl buttons and drill either two or four
holes in each. The shell dust is then swept up and used for
manure on the open fields. Williams meditates on this transformation from oyster-shell to button to shell manure:

Nature is full of astounding metamorphosis, and
assuredly that may be classed among them, when some

opposite:
London 'Pearlies'.
Pearl buttons are
sewn in elaborate
patterns on the
clothing of Pearly
Kings and Queens,
a tradition estab-
lished in the late
19th century.

particles of the little house of a mollusk on the shore of the Indian ocean, after being sown in one of the fields of England, reappear in the loaf of the cottager or the confectionary of a noble.[17]

Later in the 1890s a Japanese entrepreneur called Kokichi Mikimoto, known as the Pearl King, discovered how to mass-produce cultured pearls by injecting particles of matter into young oysters; within a few decades his pearls dominated the world cultured-pearl market as well as bringing about a transformation in the market for pearls. If until the nineteenth century strings of pearls and velvet clothes sewn with seed oysters had marked out the conspicuous consumption of the very rich, these developments in the production of cheap pearl buttons or cultured pearls made ironic imitation of extreme wealth newly possible.

One case of such use of pearls to reverse centuries-old class-specific fashions was established by London costermongers in the 1870s and '80s, decades in which trade union and workers' associations were making a substantial public presence for themselves in the streets of London in noisy and placarded marches and demonstrations. Working-class agitation for increased labour rights depended to some extent on the creation and 'performance' of mass working-class labour identity. In 1875 a municipal road-sweeper called Henry Croft began to collect the pearl buttons that had fallen to the market floor from the clothes of costermongers (market traders), stitching each by hand onto his own clothing until every inch of cloth had been covered. Dressed in this suit in order to draw attention to himself and to establish his connection with the co-operative and mutually supportive networks of the costermongers, he collected money for hospitals, orphanages and workhouses in the slums of London.

Pearly children, East End of London, 1950s.

When the costermongers joined him, each of these also put together their own suits sown in part or completely with pearl buttons, some weighing as much as 30 kilos. Soon 28 pearly 'families' had been established, one for each of the London boroughs, one for the City of Westminster, and one for the City of London. Each of these families has a Pearly Queen and King decked out on ceremonial occasions with suits sown with unique arrangements of pearl buttons.

As a marker of status, then, the pearl has been used in varied ways to mark out status and wealth. But as humans have found ways to imitate the rare natural pearls that in the fifteenth century were the motivation for so much destruction of indigenous peoples and natural resources, so artificial pearls and pearl buttons have come to be used in artful ways to challenge such cultures of conspicuous consumption.

And what of Vermeer's mysterious young woman in the turban? Where might she have acquired the pearl earring that

Spanish children wearing pearls. Alonso Sanchez Coello, *The Princesses Isobel Clara Eugenia and Catalina Micaela*, 1571, oil on canvas.

Vermeer captures as an exquisite series of colours, highlights and obscure shadows? Since a pearl this size would have been worth many times the price of the market value of any of Vermeer's paintings, it is unlikely that the painter would have passed the pair of earrings to his model as one of a series of stage props he stored in his studio. Did he borrow it? Which of Vermeer's patrons might have trusted him with a pair of earrings – or even a single earring – of such value? Was this a real pearl at all? Did Vermeer, or his model, buy one of the artificial pearls invented by a Parisian rosary-maker called M. Jacquin in Paris around this time, perhaps at a market stall in Delft? In his glass-making studio Jacquin's assistants blew tiny tear drops of glass that he filled with *l'essence d'orient*, a preparation made of white wax and the silvery scales of a river fish called *ablette*. But might not Vermeer have found this pearl simply in his imagination, conjured from the range of whites arrayed on his palette and inspired by desire to make his own *essence d'orient* in the wide eyes, turbaned head and open-mouthed mystery of the unknown girl?

Epilogue: Tonguing Oysters

For me oysters come accompanied by memory-shards of Grand Central Station in New York, where I ate oysters with my teenage son in the very early hours of an April morning, on arriving in a city whitened by a late spring snowstorm. From the taxi window, through the snow, Grand Central glowed like a stage set. Sitting on high stools at the subterranean brick-vaulted bar studded with fairy lights, we ordered Pacific oysters from a blue-painted board, oysters that had been shunted in by train from all over America with names that conjured maps and fragments of half-forgotten American history: Asharoken, Bluepoint, Buzzard Bay, Chincoteague, Fire Island, Matinecock, Mohegan, Moonstone, Westcott Bay. We played at putting oyster tastes into words as food writers do: 'briny, notes of mineral, grass and fruit . . . notes of citrus with a touch of metal . . . like licking a copper pipe'.

I began this book by claiming that the oyster's relationship to man is one of seemingly simultaneous intimacy and distance and that oysters are always frustratingly beyond words: both on the tongue and beyond the power of the tongue. Appropriately, the word 'tonguing' is used to describe what dredgers do with the tonguing tool, scraping oysters from the sea-bed as writers scrape words from memory. Oysters have been the food of the writer as well as the bohemian. Ernest Hemingway, for instance, wrote

Oysters on ice in Grand Central Station New York.

Oysters on the menu at the oyster bar at Grand Central Station in New York, April 2003.

about the emptiness finishing a story made him feel, a sadness ('as though I had made love') that only oysters could appease: 'As I ate the oysters with their strong taste of the sea and their faint metallic taste that the cold white wine washed away, leaving only the sea taste and the succulent texture, and as I drank their cold liquid from each shell and washed it down with the crisp taste of the wine, I lost the empty feeling and began to be happy and to make plans.'[1] A cartoon drawn in the 1970s shows a sleepless writer mocked by his teenage daughter as he struggles to put oysters into words through a long night.

Given the thousands of lines that oysters and pearls have inspired in writers, several poets have used oysters as a way of writing about the struggle with language itself – the problem of 'tonguing' oysters. The finest of all such poems is by Seamus

NITTY GRITTY

from *Agrippina* trans. Fiona Cleland
Methuen, 1991

Heaney and called, of course, simply 'Oysters':

Our shells clacked on the plates.
My tongue was a filling estuary,
My palate hung with starlight:
As I tasted the salty Pleiades
Orion dipped his foot into the water.
Alive and violated
They lay on their beds of ice:
Bivalves: the split bulb
And philandering sigh of the ocean.
Millions of them ripped and shucked and scattered.

We had driven to that coast through flowers and limestone
And there we were, toasting friendship,
Laying down a perfect memory
In the cool of thatch and crockery.

Over the Alps, packed deep in hay and snow,
The Romans hauled their oysters south to Rome:
I saw damp panniers disgorge

An American oyster farmer with a tonguing tool, used to scrape oysters from the sea-bed.

opposite:
Claire Bretecher, 'Nitty Gritty', a cartoon from *Agrippina* (London, 1991).

The frond-lipped, brine-strung
Glut of privilege

And I was angry that my trust could not repose
In the clear light, like poetry or freedom
Leaning in from the sea. I ate the day
Deliberately, that its tang
Might quicken me all into verb, pure verb.[2]

In post-war France, Francis Ponge (1899–1988) published *Le parti pris des choses* (*Siding with Things*), a collection of prose poems on ordinary overlooked objects including cigarettes, oranges, nails, bread, each bearing simple descriptive titles such as 'The Pleasures of the Door', 'The Mollusc', 'The Candle', 'The Crate', 'The Shrimp', 'Notes Towards a Shellfish' and 'Seashores'. The existentialist writer Albert Camus, who served with Ponge in the trenches in the First World War, called these prose poems 'an unformulated theory of absurdism' and Jean-Paul Sartre described them as an unconscious 'phenomenology'. Here is Ponge's phenomenology of the oyster:

The oyster is about as large as a medium-sized pebble, but rougher looking and less uniform in colour, brilliantly whitish. An obstinately closed world, which, however, can be opened: grasp it in the hollow of a dishcloth, use a chipped, not too sharp knife, then give it a few tries. Prying fingers cut themselves on it, and break their nails: crude work. Blows mark its envelope with white circles, sorts of halos. Inside, a whole world, both food and drink: under a firmament (strictly speaking) of mother-of-pearl, the heavens above sinking onto the heavens below form a mere puddle, a viscous, greenish sack fringed with blackish lace that ebbs and flows in your eyes and nostrils. Sometimes, though rarely, a formula purls from its nacreous throat, which is immediately used as a personal ornament.[3]

Most of Ponge's prose poems for his *Siding with Things* collection were written between 1932 and 1937, when he was working in a clerical job he called 'the penal colony' and overwhelmed by the inertia of the words used around him. He claimed he conceived a desire to reinvent language by a return to things, initiated by 'a mute supplication, mute demands' of the things themselves. Ponge's 'The oyster', like the Dutch genre paintings of the seventeenth century, appears at first glance to be simply an attempt to capture the appearance of oysters, but – also like the Dutch paintings – these words are loaded with innuendo and creative elisions and conflicts between words and metaphors which make the oyster both a creature of the vast and measureless heavens ('firmament'; 'upper and lower heavens'; 'halos'; 'a whole world') and a creature of low slime ('mere puddle'; 'greenish sack'). And there is violence here too – the cut fingers, broken nails and hammer blows.

In this 'siding with things' Ponge captures something of the borderline creature which man has made of the oyster. Over the centuries since its entry into human language the oyster has accrued multiple meanings, many of them straddling the border between seeming opposites. The oyster has spoken to man of both heavens and slime, of open and closed, of sea and land, of the microscopic and the telescopic; and in its most precious pearl, it has enshrined something of the most spectacular histories of human beauty and violence. In its resistance to language and its fascinating, closed-off yet longed-for difference, the oyster has provoked poets to produce exquisite new tonguings – frond-lipped, and brine-strung – in order to draw it into words.

Timeline of the Oyster

c. 200 MILLION BC	c. 135 MILLION BC	c. 65 MILLION BC	95 BC
Oysters evolve as some of the first bivalves in early seas	Oysters now one of the largest mollusc groups in the seas	Oysters survive the catastrophic change of climate that destroys the dinosaurs	Sergius Orata builds artificia oyster beds at Baiae; oysters become a Roman delicacy

1603	1700S	1761	1782
Elizabeth I's funeral train carries a wax effigy of the Queen covered in waxed pearls	Oysters become a delicacy of the eighteenth-century aristocratic table in Europe	Carl Linnaeus experiments with making artificial pearls	'The Poet, The Oyster and the Sensitive Plant' by William Cowper is first published, a meditation on sensitivity as a marker of the human condition

1880	1890S	1920S	1929
E. Ray Lankester uses the oyster as a moral lesson in degeneracy in *Degeneracy: A Chapter in Darwinism*	Japanese entrepreneur Kokichi Mikimoto begins mass producing artificial pearls	Oyster industries develop method of using hatcheries. Pearl ornamentation becomes fashionable in Europe because of the trade in artificial and cultured pearls	Hector Bolitho publishes *The Glorious Oyster*

c. AD 78	c. AD 600	1293	c. 1500
Romans discover British oysters on the shores of Kent and begin to carry them back to Rome across the Alps, in ice-packed baskets on the backs of donkeys	Oyster cultivation now established in China, Japan, Italy, France and Britain	Marco Polo describes the pearl-fishing trade in China	Spanish pearl trade begins, based on the Costa de las Perlas, islands off the eastern coast of Venezuela

1836	1860s	1863	1871
Oysters described as the food of the very poor in Charles Dickens's *The Pickwick Papers*	Oyster industries in Europe and America go into decline through overfishing, oyster diseases and pollution. Oyster prices start to rise	Georges Bizet's opera *The Pearl Fishers*, set off the coast of Sri Lanka, gets its first performance	Lewis Carroll publishes 'The Walrus and the Carpenter' as part of *Alice Through the Looking Glass*, a poem about human greed

1941	1969	1979	2003
M.F.K. Fisher publishes *Consider the Oyster*	Richard Burton buys the famous La Peregrina pearl for Elizabeth Taylor	Seamus Heaney publishes 'Oysters' in *Field Work*	American Boyd Bulot wins the world oyster eating record by eating 216 Louisiana oysters in 10 minutes

References

PROLOGUE

1 Hector Bolitho, *The Glorious Oyster* (London and New York, 1929), p. 4.

1 OYSTER BIOGRAPHIES

1 G. G. Simpson, *The Meaning of Evolution* (New York, 1949), p. 192.
2 C. M. Yonge, *Oysters* (London, 1960), p. 8.
3 See Zdenek, V. Spinar, *Life Before Man* (London, 1972), pp. 13–32.
4 Revd Charles Williams, *Silver-Shell; or, The Adventures of an Oyster* (London, 1856), p. 63.
5 M.F.K. Fisher, *Consider the Oyster* (New York, 1951), p. 4.
6 These objects were described and illustrated in the *Illustrated London News*, 11 August 1855.
7 Yonge, *Oysters*, p. 10.
8 Fisher, *Consider the Oyster*, p. 5.
9 Oyster sex-changes were not fully documented until 1927, when the biologist J. H. Orton conducted research, published in 1936 as 'Observations and Experiments in Sex-Change in the European Oyster (*O. edulis*), *Memoires du Musée Royale d'Histoire Naturelle de Belgique*, series 2, 3, pp. 997–1056.
10 Fisher, *Consider the Oyster*, p. 7

2 OYSTER CULTURE

1 Nicky Milner, 'Oysters, Cockles and Kitchen Middens: Changing
   Practices in the Mesolithic / Neolithic Transition', in *Consuming
   Passions and Patterns of Consumption*, ed. Preston Miracle and
   Nicky Milner (Cambridge, 2002) pp. 87–96.

2 Michael P. Richards, Paul B. Pettitt, Mary C. Stiner and Erik
   Trinkaus, 'Stable Isotope Evidence for Increasing Dietary Breadth
   in the European Mid-Upper Paleolithic', *Proceedings of the
   National Academy of Sciences*, [[AQ: OK?] xcviii/11 (22 May 2001),
   pp. 6528–32.

3 M. L. Wilson, 'Shell Middens and "Strandlopers"', *Sagittarius*,
   iv/1 (2001), pp. 1– 6.

4 Cited in Hector Bolitho, *The Glorious Oyster* (London and New
   York, 1929), p. 17.

5 Cited in Bolitho, *Glorious Oyster*, p. 19.

6 Bolitho, *Glorious Oyster*, p. 20.

7 Bolitho, *Glorious Oyster*, p. 24.

8 Bolitho, *Glorious Oyster*, p. 26.

9 Cited in Eleanor Clark, *The Oysters of Locmariaquer* (London,
   1965), p. 41.

10 See Robert Nield, *The English, the French and the Oyster* (London,
    1995), p. 90.

11 Anon., *Lucullus; or, Palatable Essays* (London, 1878) , vol. i, p. 14.

12 Richard Pinney, *Smoked Salmon and Oysters: A Feast of Suffolk
    Memories* (Orford, 1984), p. 47.

13 Pinney, *Smoked Salmon and Oysters*, p. 53.

14 David G. Gordon, Nancy E. Blanton and Terry Y. Nosho, *Heaven
    on the Half Shell: The Story of the NorthWest's Love Affair with the
    Oyster* (Washington, DC, 2001), pp. 85–7.

15 Pinney, *Smoked Salmon and Oysters*, p. 87.

1 Martial, *Epigrams*, ed. and trans. D. R. Shackleton Bailey, vol. I, Loeb Classical Library (Cambridge, MA, 1993), vol. III, p. 60. This translation comes from a website on Roman poetry: http://www.svtc.org.uk/LatinOnline/sc3/unit3/poetry1.htm

2 Cited in David Gordon, Nancy Blanton and Terry Nosho, *Heaven on the Half Shell: The Story of the Northwest's Love Affair with the Oyster* (Washington, DC, and Portland, OR, 2001), p. 17.

3 Cited in J. R. Philpotts, *Oysters and All about Them* (London, 1890), p. 59.

4 Piero Camporesi, *Exotic Brew: The Art of Living in the Age of Enlightenment*, trans. Christopher Woodall (London, 1994), p. 36.

5 Camporesi, *Exotic Brew*, pp. 38–9.

6 Camporesi, *Exotic Brew*, p. 39.

7 Henry Mayhew, *London Labour and the London Poor* (London, 1851), p. 62.

8 John J. McCusker, 'Comparing the Purchasing Power of Money in Great Britain from 1284 to any other Year including the Present', *Economic History Services*, (2001), URL: http://www.eh.net/hmit/ppowerbp/

9 Mayhew, *London Labour and the London Poor*, p. 65.

10 Mayhew, *London Labour and the London Poor*, p. 78.

11 Cited in Joseph J. Cook, *The Changeable World of the Oyster* (New York, 1974), p. 48.

12 Cook, *Changeable World of the Oyster*, p. 48.

13 James Cook, *Captain Cook's Journal during his First Voyage around the World*, chapter 8 . Online e-text: http://etext.library.adelaide.edu.au/c/c77j/chapter8.html

14 *The Letters of Charles Dickens*, ed. Humphrey House, Graham Storey and Kathleen Tillotson (Oxford, 1974), vol. III, p. 244.

15 D. Cannadine 'Civic Ritual and the Colchester Oyster Feast', *Past*

& *Present*, xcv (1982), pp. 107–30.

16 Gurney Benham, *Colchester Oyster Feast* (Colchester, 1902), p. 14.

17 Eleanor Clark, *The Oysters of Locmariaquer* (London, 1965), p. 178.

18 George Augustus Sala, *Twice around the Clock; or, The Hours of the Day and Night in London* (London, 1859), p. 319.

19 Sala, *Twice around the Clock*, p. 327.

20 Robert Nield, *The English, the French and the Oyster* (London, 1995), p. 151.

21 Michael Peppiatt, *Francis Bacon: Anatomy of an Enigma* (New York, 1996), p. 47.

4 OYSTERS AND GLUTTONY

1 Norman B. Spector, trans., *The Complete Fables of Jean de la Fontaine* (Chicago, 1999), p. 54.

2 Samuel Bowden, *Poems on Various Subjects* (London, 1754), pp. 8–9.

3 *The Letters of Charles Dickens*, ed. Humphrey House, Graham Storey and Kathleen Tillotson (Oxford, 1974), vol. III, pp. 291–2.

4 *Punch*, 11 January 1868.

5 J. R. Philpotts, *Oysters and All about Them* (London, 1890), pp. 781–2.

6 Geoffrey Pike, John Cann and Roger Lambert, *Oysters and Dredgermen* (London, 1992), p. 14.

7 See Rebecca Stott, *Darwin and the Barnacle* (London, 2003), chapters 2 and 3.

8 *Minutes of Evidence Taken before the Select Committee on Oyster Fisheries* (6 April 1876), p. 114: Mr F. Pennell.

9 I am indebted to the scrupulous research of Matthew Demakos, who has explored the origins of and sources for 'The Walrus and the Carpenter' in an unpublished text called *The Annotated Walrus*.

10 Martin Gardner, *The Annotated Alice* (London, 1970), p. 237.

5 OYSTER FLESH

1 A. Fishe Shelly Esq. [James Watson Gerard], *Ostrea; or, The Loves of the Oysters* (New York, 1857), p. 17.
2 Guillaume Figuier, *The Ocean World* (London, 1868), p. 379.
3 See Peter Hulme, *Colonial Encounters: Europe and the Native Caribbean, 1492–1797* (New York and London, 1986), and William Arens, *The Man-Eating Myth: Anthropology and Anthropophagy* (New York, 1979).
4 Translated into English in 1603.
5 Robert Boyle, 'Reflection III: Upon the Eating of Oysters', in *Occasional Reflections*, vol. v of *The Works of Robert Boyle*, ed. Michael Hunter and Edward B. Davis (London, 1999), pp. 169–72.
6 Jeremy Bentham, *Introduction to the Principles of Morals and Legislation* (Oxford, 1781), p. 311.
7 Robert Grant, 'Observations and Experiments on the Structure and Functions of the Sponge', *Edinburgh Philosophical Journal*, XIV/27 (1826), p. 123.
8 'The Poet, the Oyster and the Sensitive Plant', in *The Works of William Cowper* (London, 1835–7), pp. 348–50.
9 Cited in J. R. Philpotts, *Oysters and All about Them* (London, 1890), pp. 221–2.
10 Chauncey M. Depew, *My Memories of Eighty Years* (New York and London, 1922), chapter 23.
11 Julia Kristeva, *Powers of Horror*, trans. Leon S. Roudiez (Columbia, NY 1982), pp. 1, 2 and 4.
12 Kristeva, *Powers of Horror*, p. 75.
13 Anne Stevenson, 'Oysters' from *Granny Scarecrow* (London, 2000), p. 53.

6 OYSTER PHILOSOPHIES

1 A. Fishe Shelly, Esq. [James Watson Gerard], *Ostrea; or, The Loves of Oysters* (New York, 1857), p. 15.
2 Cited in Hector Bolitho, *The Glorious Oyster* (London and New York, 1929), p. 115.
3 Cited in Bolitho, *Glorious Oyster*, p. 60. The poet was a member of the Preston 'Oyster and Parched Pea Club' and the poem was published in 1816.
4 Edward Forbes, 'Shellfish: Their Ways and Works', *Westminster Review*, LVII (January 1852), pp. 44–5.
5 'The Happy Fishing-Ground', *All the Year Round*, XI/161 (26 November 1859).
6 Revd Charles Williams, *Silver-Shell; or, The Adventures of an Oyster* (London, 1856), p. 159.
7 Jane Welsh Carlyle, *Letters and Memorials of Jane Welsh Carlyle*, ed. James Anthony Froude (London, 1883), vol. III, p. 21. I am grateful to Ellen Jordan of the University of Newcastle, Australia, for this reference.
8 E. Ray Lankester, *Degeneration: A Chapter in Darwinism* (London, 1880), p. 33.

7 OYSTER ARTS

1 Liana de Girolami Cheney, 'The Oyster in Dutch Genre Paintings: Moral or Erotic Symbolism?', *Artibus et Historiae*, XV (1987), pp. 135–58.
2 Svetlana Alpers, *The Art of Describing: Dutch Art in the Seventeenth Century* (London, 1983), p. 91.
3 Francis Bacon, *Works*, ed. James Spedding, Robert Leslie and Douglas Denon Heath (London, 1996), vol. IV, p. 13.
4 Norman Bryson, *Looking at the Overlooked* (London, 1990), p. 61.
5 Mark Doty, *Still Life with Oysters and Lemon* (Boston, MA, 2001), p. 15.

6 Doty, *Still Life with Oysters and Lemon*, p. 16

7 Doty, *Still Life with Oysters and Lemon*, p. 8.

8 Doty, *Still Life with Oysters and Lemon*, p. 67.

9 Nancy Princenthal, 'Bianca Sforni at Paul Kasmin', *Art in America*, LXXXIV (June 1996), pp. 97–8.

10 Paul Hill's work can be seen at his website: http://www.absolutearts.com/metalforms/

11 http://www.acfnewsource.org/art/art_on_half_shell.html

8 OYSTERS, SEX AND SEDUCTION

1 M.F.K. Fisher, *Consider the Oyster* (New York, 1941), p. 64.

2 Cited in *An Account of the Grand Oyster Demonstration at the Theatre Royal Preston and the Celebrated Oration by Professor Blezard* (London, 1862), p. 16.

3 Michael Ondaatje, *Coming through Slaughter* (London, 1979), p. 9.

4 Anon., *Lucullus; or, Palatable Essays*, 2 vols (London, 1878), p. 20.

5 William Makepeace Thackeray, 'Ottilia', in *The Fitz-boodle Papers*, vol. IV of the Oxford Thackeray (1908).

6 A. Fishe Shelly [James Watson Gerard], *Ostrea; or, The Loves of Oysters* (New York, 1857), pp. 22, 23, 26 and 35.

7 Sarah Waters, *Tipping the Velvet* (London, 1999), p. 4.

8 Bertrand Davis, 'Mine Oyster and the Story of Its Pearl', *Harmondsworth Magazine*, III (August 1999), pp. 53–8.

9 Anthony Bourdain, *Kitchen Confidential: Adventures in the Culinary Underbelly* (London, 2000), pp. 16–17.

9 PEARL

1 Walter Liedtke, *Vermeer and the School of Delft* (New Haven, CT, 2002), p. 166.

2 M.F.K. Fisher, *Consider the Oyster* (New York, 1941), p. 49.

3 H. Martyn Hart, *The World of the Sea* (London, 1869), p. 40.

4 Cited in George Frederick Kunz and Charles Hugh Stevenson, *The Book of the Pearl: The History, Art, Science and Industry of the Queen of Gems* (1908; New York, 1993), p. 158.

5 Pliny the Elder, *Natural History*, ed. and trans. R. Rackham, W.H.S. Jones and D. E. Eichholz (London, 1961–8), vol. III, pp. 235–7.

6 Richard Pulteney, *General View of the Writings of Linnaeus* (London, 1805), p. 47.

7 Cited in Kristin Joyce and Shellei Addison, *Pearls: Ornament and Obsession* (London, 1992), p. 36.

8 'Transmigrations' (1839) in *James Montgomery: The Poetical Works* (London, 1850), p. 363.

9 Cited in Joyce and Addison, *Pearls*, p. 86.

10 Cited in Joyce and Addison, *Pearls*, p. 94.

11 Montaigne, *Essays*, trans. John Florio (1603), ed. J.I.M. Stewart (London, 1931), p. 314.

12 Cited in Kunz and Stevenson, *The Book of the Pearl*, p. 454.

13 Johann Georg Kohl, *Reisen in Südrussland* (Leipzig, 1846), vol. I, p. 15.

14 Cited in Joyce and Addison, *Pearls*, p. 115.

15 Kunz and Stevenson, *The Book of the Pearl*, p. 109.

16 Revd Charles Williams, *Silver-Shell; or, The Adventures of an Oyster* (London, 1856), p. 90.

17 Williams, *Silver-Shell*, pp. 91–2.

EPILOGUE

1 Ernest Hemingway, *A Moveable Feast* (New York, 1964), p. 13.

2 Seamus Heaney, 'Oysters', from *Field Work* (London, 1979), p. 3.

3 From Francis Ponge, *Selected Poems* (London, 1998), p. 26, copyright Gallimard (1942). *Le partis pris des choses (Siding with Things)*, trans. C. K. Williams and Wake Forest University Press (Winston-Salem, 1994).

Bibliography

Bergstrom, Ingvar, *Dutch Still-Life Painting in the Seventeenth Century*, trans. Christina Hedstrom and Gerald Taylor (London, 1956)

Bleazard, Robert, *An Account of the Oyster Demonstration at the Theatre Royal, Preston* (London, 1862)

Bolitho, Hector, *The Glorious Oyster* (London and New York, 1929)

Brooks, William K., *The Oyster: A Popular Summary of a Scientific Study* (Baltimore, 1905, reprinted 1996)

Clark, Eleanor, *The Oysters of Locmariaquer* (London, 1965)

Collard, Allen Ovenden, *The Oyster & Dredgers of Whitstable* (London, 1902).

Cook, Joseph J., *The Changeable World of the Oyster* (New York, 1974)

Dakin W. J., *Pearls* (New York, 1913)

Donkin, R. A., *Beyond Price: Pearls and Pearl Fishing: Origins to the Age of Discoveries* (Philadelphia, 1998)

Doty, Mark, *Still Life with Oysters and Lemon* (Boston, MA, 2001)

Figuer, G. L., *The Ocean World; Being a Descriptive History of the Sea and its Inhabitants* (London, 1868)

Fishe Shelly A. [James Watson Gerard], *Ostrea; or, The Love of Oysters* (New York, 1857)

Fisher, Mary Frances Kennedy, *Consider the Oyster* (New York, 1941)

Forbes, Edward, 'Shell-fish: Their Ways and Works', *Westminster Review*, LVII (January 1852), pp. 42–61

Freeman, Sarah, *Mutton and Oysters: The Victorians and their Food* (London, 1989)

Gordon, David G., Nancy E. Blanton and Terry Y. Nosho, *Heaven on the Half Shell: The Story of the NorthWest's Love Affair with the Oyster* (Washington, DC, 2001)

Hall, Herbert Byng, *The Oyster; Where, How, and When to Find, Breed, Cook and Eat It* (London, 1861)

Joyce, Kristin, and Shellei Addison, *Pearls: Ornament & Obsession*, introduction by Sumiko Mikimoto (London, 1992)

Kunz, George Frederick, and Charles Hugh Stevenson, *The Book of the Pearl: The History, Art, Science and Industry of the Queen of Gems* (New York, 1908; reprinted 1993)

Line, Shirley, *A Passion for Oysters: The Art of Eating and Enjoying* (London, 1995)

Neild, Robert, *The English, The French and the Oyster* (London, 1995)

Pankow, F.H.E., *The Mollusc Paramount: Being Valuable & Interesting Information about Oysters* (London and Dunstable, 1909)

Philpotts, John Richard, *Oysters and All about Them: A Complete History of the Titular Subject Exhaustive on All Points of Necessary and Curious Information from the Earliest Writers to Those of the Present Time, with Numerous Additions, Facts and Notes* (London, 1890)

Pike, Geoffrey, John Cann and Roger Lambert, *Oysters and Dredgermen* (Whistable, 1992)

Pinney, Richard, *Smoked Salmon and Oysters: A Feast of Suffolk*

Memories (Orford, 1984)

Ponge, Francis 'The Oyster' from *Selected Poems* (London, 1998)

Romero, Aldemaro, Susanna Chilbert and M. G. Eisenhart, 'Cubagua's Pearl-Oyster Beds: The First Depletion of a Natural Resource Caused by Europeans in the American Continent', *Journal of Political Ecology*, VI (1999), pp. 57–78

Rydon, John, *Oysters with Love with Drawings by Don Roberts* (London, 1968)

Wennerster, John R., *The Oyster Wars of Chesapeake Bay* (Centreville, 1981)

Wilkins, Noel P., *Squires, Spalpeens and Spats: Oysters and Oystering in Galway Bay* (Galway, 2001)

Williams, Revd Charles, *Silver-Shell; or, the Adventures of an Oyster* (London, 1856)

Yonge, Charles Maurice, *Oysters* (London, 1960)

Oyster Recipes

There are many oyster recipes from different periods of history and from round the world. This is a selection of some of the more famous or unusual ones.

OYSTERS EN BROCHETTE

1½ tablespoons salt
1½ teaspoons garlic powder
1½ teaspoons sweet paprika
1¼ teaspoons cayenne pepper
1 teaspoon black pepper
¾ teaspoon white pepper
¾ teaspoon onion powder
¾ teaspoon oregano
½ teaspoon dried thyme
¼ teaspoon dried basil
¾ pound (approx.) sliced bacon, cut into 2½ inch pieces
12 mushrooms
5 dozen medium to large shucked oysters (about 2¾ pounds)
¾ cup of all-purpose flour
   vegetable oil for frying

Combine salt, seasonings and pepper in a bowl. Set aside. Blanch bacon pieces in boiling water about 4 minutes. Rinse in cold water and drain. Place ingredients on 9- to 10-inch metal or wooden skewers as follows: one mushroom cap, then one piece of bacon and one oyster. Mix the seasonings with the flour. Heat oil in a heavy frying pan. Just before frying, dredge each skewer well in seasoned flour, shaking off excess. Fry each skewer in hot oil until golden brown and crispy, about 2 to 3 minutes per side. Drain before serving. Makes 6 servings.

OYSTER STEW

¼ pint of cold water
3 dozen small to medium oysters
¼ pound unsalted butter
1 handful of finely chopped celery
½ teaspoon cayenne pepper
¼ teaspoon white pepper
¼ teaspoon salt
1 finely chopped green onion
1 small pot of double cream

Add water to the oysters and refrigerate for at least 1 hour. Strain and reserve oysters and oyster water. Refrigerate until ready to use. In a large frying pan, combine butter, celery, peppers, salt and quarter of a pint of the oyster water. Cook over high heat for 3 minutes, shaking the pan almost constantly. Add remaining ½ cup of oyster water and continue cooking and shaking the pan for 1 minute. Stir in green onions. Gradually add cream, whisking constantly. Bring the mixture to the boil, whisking almost constantly. Add oysters and cook just until they curl, about 2 to 4 minutes, whisking constantly. Remove from heat and serve, stirring as you ladle portions. Makes 4 main course or 8 appetizer servings.

BROILED OYSTERS IN CHAMPAGNE SAUCE

24 shucked oysters on the half shell
2 tablespoons butter
1½ tablespoons flour
    pint of champagne or dry white wine
    Pinch of cayenne pepper
    salt, to taste
    coarse salt or seaweed

Strain oyster liquor through cheesecloth and reserve ½ cup. Discard the rest. In a small saucepan, melt butter over medium heat. Add flour, stir and cook, stirring occasionally, 2 to 3 minutes. Slowly add oyster liquor, stirring to remove lumps. Add champagne and stir. Add cayenne and salt and stir until thickened and blended. Cool slightly. Preheat broiler/grill. Nestle opened oysters on bed of seaweed or coarse salt on cookie sheet or baking pan. Top each oyster with a spoonful of sauce. Broil/grill about 4 to 6 inches from heat source just until sauce begins to colour, about 2 minutes. Makes 4 to 6 appetizer servings.

ANGELS ON HORSEBACK

This recipe was popular in the nineteenth century. Open as many oysters as you will need, reserving the liquid. Wrap each oyster in a slice of bacon and secure with a toothpick. Cook under a grill or on the barbecue, turning until the bacon is crispy. Remove from the heat and roll in fine fried breadcrumbs. Serve on toast with a garnish of watercress.

OYSTERS KILPATRICK

24 large oysters
4   rashers of rindless streaky bacon, very finely chopped
    Worcestershire sauce

Line a baking tray with coarse salt. Carefully open the oysters,
leaving them on the half-shell. Nestle them into the salt. Scatter
bacon onto each oyster, and sprinkle with a few drops of
Worcestershire sauce. Grill just until the oysters are hot and the
bacon is crisp. Serve immediately. Serves 4.

OYSTERS A L'INDIENNE

24 oysters
    bacon
    cloves
2   tablespoons of chutney sauce
2   tablespoons of Worcestershire sauce
1   tablespoon minced parsley
6   olives
½   teaspoon of paprika

Drain large oysters, wipe them dry, wrap each in a slice of
bacon, fastened with a toothpick, and stick two cloves in each
oyster. Mix the chutney sauce, Worcestershire sauce, minced
parsley, olives cut fine, and paprika. Put the oysters in the pan
and cook until the bacon is crisp and the oysters plump. Pour
the sauce mixture over the oysters, stirring it thoroughly into
the gravy. This will serve 3 or 4.

OYSTERS ROCKEFELLER

1   pound of fresh spinach
12 oysters, opened with juice reserved
6   finely chopped shallots
2   cloves of garlic, crushed
2   tablespoons of butter
1   heaped tablespoon of heavy cream
1   tablespoon of Pernod
    a pinch of hot-pepper flakes or teaspoon of hot pepper
    sauce
    a handful of grated Gruyère cheese
    ground black pepper

Wash the fresh spinach and steam for 3 to 4 minutes until just cooked. Drain and squeeze out the liquid. Chop finely. Arrange the oysters on a flat, non-stick baking dish. Sauté the shallots and garlic in the butter, add the spinach, oyster juice and pepper. Add the cream and bring to a simmer. Purée the mixture in a blender. Return to a clean pan. Add the Pernod and pepper flakes or sauce. Heat gently, stirring occasionally. Spoon the mixture over each oyster and then sprinkle with the cheese. Place under a grill until the cheese sizzles. Serve immediately. Serves 2.

CARPET-BAG STEAK

Steak filled with oysters spilling out of a pocket cut into the flesh was said to resemble a carpet bag. This recipe is from Louis Diat, *Cooking à la Ritz* (New York: J.B. Lippincott & Co., 1941).

Using steak cut from the sirloin 1½ to 2 inches thick, cut through the centre to make a pocket. Stuff the pocket with raw oysters, seasoned with salt and pepper. Sew the edges of the pocket together. Broil/grill for about 15 minutes on each side. Serve with potatoes.

A Selection of Oyster Bars and Restaurants

ENGLAND

Kent

Wheeler's Oyster Bar
8 High Street
Whitstable
01227-273311

Whistable Oyster Fishery Restaurant
17–20 Sea Street
Whitstable
01227-276856

Denny's Lobster and Oyster Bar
3 Station Approach
Chislehurst
020-8467-5612

Suffolk

The Butley-Orford Oysterage
Market Hill
Orford
Woodbridge
01394-450277

London

Bibendum Oyster Bar
Michelin Building
81 Fulham Road, SW3
020-7589-1480

Green's Restaurant and Oyster Bar
36 Duke Street, SW1
020-7930-4566

Randall & Aubin
16 Brewer Street, W1
020-7287-4447

J. Sheekey
28–32 St Martin's Court, WC2
020-7240-2565

The Rib Room and Oyster Bar
Hyatt Carlton Tower
Cadogan Place, SW1
020-7858-7053

Wheeler's
12a Duke of York Street, SW1
020-7930-2460

Loch Fyne Oyster Restaurants
Head Office
175 Hampton Road
Twickenham
Middlesex
020-8404-6686

Branches in London at Chalk Farm, Covent
Garden, Fulham Road, Barnet, Egham,
Elton, Loughton, Twickenham; elsewhere
in England at Bath, Beaconsfield, Brighton,
Bristol, Cambridge, Harrogate, Henley-on-
Thames, Knowle, Norwich, Nottingham,
Oxford, Portsmouth, Reading, Sevenoaks,
Tunbridge Wells, Winchester

SCOTLAND

Café Royal Oyster Bar Restaurant
17–17a West Register Street
Edinburgh
0131-556-4124

The Loch Fyne Oyster Bar
Cairndow
Argyll
01499-600236

Oyster Restaurant
Strand Road
Rosslare
County Wexford
053-32439

Oyster Tavern
The Spa
Tralee
County Kerry
066-7136102

The Whistling Oyster
Main Street
Bundoran
County Donegal
353-7241490

USA

New York City

Aquagrill
210 Spring Street
Manhattan
212-274-0505

Balthazar,
80 Spring Street
Manhattan
212-965-1414

Blue Fin
1567 Broadway (Midtown West)
Manhattan
212-918-1400

Blue Ribbon Brooklyn
280 Fifth Avenue
Brooklyn
212-840-0404

Blue Ribbon Manhattan
97 Sullivan Street
Manhattan
212-274-0404

Grand Central Oyster Bar and Restaurant
Grand Central Terminal
89 East 42nd Street
Manhattan
212-490-6650

Jack's Luxury Oyster Bar
246 East 5th Street
Manhattan
212-673-0338

Pearl Oyster Bar
18 Cornelia Street
Manhattan
212-691-8211

California

Brigantine – Coronado
1333 Orange Avenue
Coronado
619-435-4166

PJ's Oyster Bed
737 Irving Street
San Francisco
415-566-7775

Swan Oyster Depot
1517 Polk Street
San Francisco
415-673-1101

Florida

City Oyster
213 East Atlantic Avenue
Delray Beach
561-272-0220

Illinois

Bluepoint Oyster Bar
741 West Randolph Street
Chicago
312-207-1222

Louisiana

Black's Oyster Bar
319 Père Megret Street
Abbeville
337-893-4266

Acme Seafood and Oyster House
724 Iberville Street
New Orleans
504-522-5973

Casamento's Restaurant
4330 Magazine Street
New Orleans
504-895-9761

Massachusetts

B&G Oysters
550 Tremont Street
Boston
617-423-0550

McCormick & Schmicks
Faneuil Hall Marketplace
Boston
617-720-5522

Union Oyster House
41 Union Street
Boston
617-227-2750

The Oyster Cabin
785 Quaker Highway Route 146A
Uxbridge
508-278-4440

North Carolina

T. & W. Oyster Bar
Highway 58 North
Cape Carteret
252-393-8838

Half Shell Oyster Bar and Seafood
Restaurant
1706 Battleground Avenue
Greensboro
336-274-0950

42nd Street Oyster Bar

508 West Jones Street
Raleigh
919-831-2811

Virginia

22nd Street Oyster Bar
2200 Colonial Avenue
Norfolk
757-248-2403

Washington

Oyster Bay Inn and Restaurant
4412 Kitsap Way
Bremerton
360-377-5510

Elliott's Oyster House
1201 Alaskan Way, Pier 56
Seattle
206-623-4340

AUSTRALIA

Blue Oyster
2-22B/12 Knox
Double Bay
New South Wales
02-9362-4010

The Melbourne Oyster Bar and Seafood
Restaurant
209 King Street
Melbourne
Victoria
03-9670-1881

Tommy Ruff's Seafood and Oyster Bar
56 Marina Boulevard
Cullen Bay
Northern Territory
08-8981-3633

CANADA

Naked Oyster
110 Dundas Street

London
Ontario
519-667-1337

FRANCE

Paris

(Most brasseries in Paris serve oysters, displayed outside at the entrance.)

Brasserie Le Dôme
108 boulevard du Montparnasse
01-43-35-2581

L'Ecailler du Bistrot
22 rue Paul Bert
01-43-72-7677

L'Huitrier
16 rue Saussier Leroy
01-40-54-8344

Le Wepler
14 place de Clichy
01-45-22-5324

Marseilles

Coquillages Toinou
3 cours Saint-Louis
04-91-33-1494

Nice

Grand Café de Turin
5 place Garibaldi
04-93-62-2952

JAPAN

Tokyo

Ginza Bairin
Kojunsya Street
7-8-1 Ginza
Chuo-ku
03-3571-0350

Ginza Sembikiya 3F Restaurant
8-8-8 Ginza
Chuo-ku
03-3572-0105

Kitchen Yanagi
Nodaya Building
8-6-19 Ginza
Chuo-ku
03-3572-7277

Mikawaya Honten
4-7-16 Ginza
Chuo-ku
03-3561-2006

Mikawaya Melsa Store (New Melsa Store 7F)
5-7-12 Ginza
Chuo-ku
03-3574-8075

Rengatei
3-5-16 Ginza
Chuo-ku
03-3561-7258

Restaurant Jardan
3-3-13 Ginza
Chuo-ku
03-3562-1691

Acknowledgements

For the generous gathering of oyster ephemera from archives, books and galleries around the world I would like to thank Kevin Jackson, Jonathan Burt, Patricia Fara and the members of the Victoria List, particularly Ellen Jordan and Matt Demakos. For patient and inspired picture research and editorial work I would like to thank Amanda Randall, Robbie Kneale and Jane Seakins, talented undergraduate students at APU, Cambridge. Thank you to Hannah Morrish for helping with the index. The pictures were funded by a grant from the British Academy, for which I am most grateful.

Photo Acknowledgements

The author and publishers wish to express their thanks to the below sources of illustrative material and/or permission to reproduce it:

The Art Institute of Chicago (Arthur Jerome Eddy Memorial Collection), photo © 2000 The Art Institute of Chicago, All Rights Reserved: p. 129; photos by the author, or from the author's collection: pp. 32, 35, 41, 47, 67, 72, 79, 89, 98, 99, 119, 199, 205, 207; photos courtesy of Bettman/CORBIS: pp. 85, 112; Bodleian Library, Oxford (MS Bodley 264, f. 218r), photo Bodleian Library: p. 176; from William K. Brooks, *The Oyster* (Baltimore, Maryland, 1891): pp. 44, 46, 53; photos Cambridge University Library: pp. 42, 68; from Victor Coste's *Voyage d'Exploration sur Le Littoral de la France et de l'Italie* (Paris, 1855): p. 43; photo by permission of the John Deakin Archive: p. 81; photos courtesy of the photographer, Alan Donaldson: p. 123; photos courtesy of the Mary Evans Picture Library: pp. 55, 62, 63, 69, 159; photo courtesy of the Florida State Archives: p.36; photos courtesy of Getty Images: pp. 9 (Stone), 120, 161, 202 (all Hulton Archive); photo courtesy of the artist (Paul Hill): p. 147; photo Kobal Collection/Superstock: p. 190; Koninklijk Museum voor Schone Kunsten, Antwerp, photo courtesy of the Koninklijk Museum: p. 132; Library of Congress Prints and

Photographs Division (LC-USZ6-1306), photograph by Lewis Wickes Hine: p. 6; photo courtesy of the London Pearly Kings and Queens Society: p. 201; Manchester City Art Gallery, photo Manchester City Art Galleries: p. 179; photo courtesy of The Mariner's Museum, Newport News, Virginia: p. 91; photo courtesy of Maryland Sea Grant: p. 24; The Metropolitan Museum of Art, New York (purchase), photo: © 1983 Metropolitan Museum of Art: p. 142; The Minneapolis Institute of Arts (bequest of Richard P. Gale); photo courtesy of the Minneapolis Institute of Arts: p. 194; Musée Condé, Chantilly (photo RMN-Harry Bréjat): p. 59; Musée du Louvre, Paris, photo courtesy of the Photographic Library of the Reunion des Musées Nationaux: p. 141; Museo Nacional del Prado, Madrid: pp. 136, 203; Museum Boijmans van Beuningen, Rotterdam: p. 139; National Gallery, London (photo National Gallery Picture Library). p. 58. National Gallery of Art, Washington, DC (Patrons Permanent Fund), photo Bob Grove/National Gallery of Art Office of Visual Services: p. 137; photos courtesy of the National Library of Australia, Sydney: pp. 151, 152; National Portrait Gallery, London, photo National Portrait Gallery Picture Library, by courtesy of the National Portrait Gallery, London: p. 187; photos courtesy of Pacific Coast Shellfish Growers Association: pp. 14, 28, 45, 48, 50, 51, 52, 156; photo courtesy of Popperfoto: p. 80; photo courtesy of Anthony Redpath/CORBIS, p. 173; from Lovell Augustus Reeve and G. B. Sowerby, *Monograph of the Genus Philine* (London, 1873): pp. 18, 20, 21, 22, 23; photos courtesy of the artist (Philip Ross): pp. 148, 149; Royal Cabinet of Paintings, 'Mauritshuis', The Hague, photos courtesy of the 'Mauritshuis': pp. 134, 135, 172; photo courtesy of the artist (Bianca Sforni): p. 144; Staatsgalerie, Stuttgart, photo courtesy of the Staatsgalerie: p. 169; photo courtesy of the artist (Stephen Turner): p. 150; photo courtesy

Index